D0012494

Rubén Martínez

THE OTHER SIDE

Rubén Martínez is a journalist and poet.
He is a news editor at *L.A. Weekly*.

THE OTHER SIDE

THE OTHER SIDE

*Notes from the New L.A.,
Mexico City, and Beyond*

Rubén Martínez

VINTAGE DEPARTURES
VINTAGE BOOKS
A DIVISION OF RANDOM HOUSE, INC.
NEW YORK

FIRST VINTAGE DEPARTURES EDITION, MAY 1993

Copyright © 1992 by Verso

All rights reserved under International and Pan-American
Copyright Conventions. Published in the United States by
Vintage Books, a division of Random House, Inc., New York,
and distributed in Canada by Random House of Canada
Limited, Toronto. Originally published in hardcover in Great
Britain and in the United States by Verso, London, in 1992.

Library of Congress Cataloging-in-Publication Data
Martínez, Rubén
    Notes from the New L.A., Mexico City, and Beyond /
Rubén Martínez.
        p.   cm. — (Vintage departures)
    Originally published: London: Verso, 1992
    ISBN 0-679-74591-2
    1. Hispanic Americans—California—Los Angeles.
2. Politics and culture —California—Los Angeles.
3. Los Angeles (Calif.)—Popular culture.
4. Los Angeles (Calif.)—Politics and government.
I. Title
F869.L89S756   1993
979.4'9400468—dc20   92-50704   CIP

Author photograph © Ted Soqui

Manufactured in the United States of America
10   9   8   7   6   5   4   3   2   1

Contents

Acknowledgments

Versions of "The Other Side," "Talkin' 'Bout My Generation," "Tijuana Burning," "Going Up in L.A.," "A Festival of Moments," and "A Death in the Family," first appeared in the *L.A. Weekly*. "Homecoming" appeared in *Enclitic* magazine. "There's a War" appeared in *Rohwedder International Quarterly*. "Manifesto" appeared in *Harbinger: Fiction and Poetry by Los Angeles Writers*. "Generation" appeared in *Invocation L.A.: Urban Multicultural Poetry* (West End Press). Portions of the "L.A. Journal" appeared in *Sex, Death and God in L.A.* (Pantheon Books).

For their support and inspiration, I would like to thank: Mike Davis, Colin MacLeod, Yadira Arévalo, Lynell George, Kit Rachlis and the *L.A. Weekly* crew, Guillermo Gómez-Peña, Emily Hicks, Hugo Sánchez, Marco Vinicio González, María Eraña, Elia Arce, Joaquín Meza, Salvador Juárez, Patricia Campos Cisneros, Francisco Rivera, Ricardo Ventura, Michelle Clinton, José García, Ana María García, John Oliver Simon, Juan Felipe Herrera, Hans-Jürgen Schacht, Carmelo Alvarez, K2S–STN, Daniel Lara, Arturo Olivas, Dr. Rudy Acuña, Dr. Marta López-Garza, Ted Soqui, Pedro Meyer, Marcus Kuiland-Nazario, Jack Grapes, David Reid, Jane Walker, Maldita Vecindad, Marusa Reyes, Mike Sprinker, Fr Luis Olivares, Fr Michael Kennedy, and the Poets Beyond Madness at Hollenbeck Junior High School in East Los Angeles.

Sources of the photographs are as follows: Border Crossing by Ted Soqui; Rubén Darío Building by Rubén Martínez; Salvage Work by Rubén Martínez; Baptism, family photo; Family in San Salvador, family photo;

Olivares by José Galvez; Cruising Havana by Enrique Berumen; Latino AIDS Vigil by Ted Soqui; Homeless Sleeping at La Placita by José Galvez; Aztec Nation by Ted Soqui; Performance by Rubén Martínez; Burning the Mono by Carmela Castrejón; Grandparents, family photo; The Paris Inn, family photo; Prime by Ted Soqui; Never Been Caught by Pedro Meyer; The Belmont Tunnel by Ted Soqui; Kings Stop at Nothing by Pedro Meyer; K2S–STN by Ted Soqui; L.A. Festival by Ted Soqui; Security Measures by Ted Soqui; Cristo by Rubén Martínez; Maldita Vecindad by Maldita Vecindad; Prayer Before Dinner by José Galvez.

Para Y, a pesar de la distancia,
y para mi familia

THE OTHER SIDE

EL OTRO LADO
Border Crossing

The Other Side

From Elvis to Fidel to Vietnam to Allende to L.A.'s eternal HOLLYWOOD dream-lie to the shell-shocked *barrios* of Central America; and the flames leaping skyward from Watts, and the tear-gas canister that blew off Rubén Salazar's head outside the Silver Dollar Saloon on a hot August East L.A. afternoon when the Chicano Moratorium met its end, and the JFK/RFK assassination scenes playing over and over in my mind . . . shots ringing out, explosions that shook my childhood awake to the ways of the world: dreams are blown away, dreams are blown away, dreams are blown . . . these were the years of snapping in two, of fearing the Big One, "The End" that Jim Morrison sang of, Charles Manson lurking in the shadows of Flower Power.

The 1960s are still etched into my memory, snapshots culled from the mass media's collective conscience that appear alongside my recollection of the seventies and eighties, even though I'm not a member of the Flower Power generation. Mine is the generation that arrived too late for Che Guevara but too early for the fall of the Berlin Wall. Weaned on a blend of cultures, languages, and ideologies (Anglo/Latino, Spanish/English, individualist/collectivist), I have lived both in the North and the South over my twenty-nine years, trying to be South in the South, North in the North, South in the North and North in the South. Now, I stand at the center—watching history whirl around me as my own history fissures: my love shatters, North and South, and a rage arises from within as the ideal of existential unity crumbles. I cannot tell whether what I see is a beginning or an end. My quest for a true center, for a cultural, political and romantic home, is stripped of direction.

3

The eye of the hurricane is Los Angeles and I return to the religious ritual of the Catholic Mass to find the home within me that would in turn help open a path through the colliding signs outside. I *must* hold on to some hope: that the many selves can find some kind of form together without annihilating one another. As the world must mend, but within the mending there is still war, and the echoes of the repressions are loud still.

I told myself that by the time I was thirty, I would be a world traveler, healing the wounds between cultures, between ideologies, between selves and others, and sign treaties with my various selves—Mexican, Salvadoran, middle-class Angeleno, *barrio* dweller, poet, journalist, et cetera. As I take stock, I admit that whatever treaties were signed over the years were fragile, perhaps artificial. The rage I speak of—the frustration that lies between the ideal and the awareness of its impossibility—lashes out to destroy every dream I've ever begun.

I give thanks, however, that I was born at a time when I could live so many realities at once: that I could sit in a San Salvador café and argue about a new language with poets who survived the death squads and with the ghosts of those who didn't. And that I could be in San Salvador in Los Angeles by hanging out in Little Central America, and in Los Angeles in Mexico City by dancing to the rhythms of its underground rock 'n' roll. I give thanks, in a Catholic way, because this coming together is much like a crucifixion—each encounter signifies a contradiction, a cross: the contrary signs battle each other without end, a battle that seems as eternal as the one between spirit and flesh. One can spy on multilingual store signs in New York or Los Angeles, eat food from all over the world, listen to the rhythms of every culture and time on the airwaves, but the fires of nationalism still rage, and in the cities of the United States, blacks and Koreans and Latinos and Anglos live in anything but a multicultural paradise. As for myself, it is all too often that I yearn for the Other even when I am with the Other: nowhere do I feel complete.

With the walls coming down, it may be possible that I'll be able to see beyond the ruins. Gaze upon the other side and see the others—clearly. The chronicles that comprise this book record a search for the home that I've lost and found countless times over the past five years. It has been, it is, in other words, a search for a one that is much more than two. Because, wherever I am now, I must be much more than two. I must be North and South in the North and in the South . . .

The Winds of October

San Salvador, October 10, 1986

"Get out or we'll get you," the voice on the phone had said. There was silence for a few seconds, and then . . . *click*. Raúl knew that he couldn't take the threat lightly—several of his fellow activists had been rounded up by the security forces in recent weeks. Some were recognized as prisoners by the authorities. Others . . . who knew about their whereabouts?

Raúl went over a last-minute mental checklist for the trip to Mexico as he and Aída walked in silence down the steps from San Salvador's National Library. The sky was dotted with clouds, the air slightly humid from last night's storm, but there was a tinge of summer on the light breeze. Over the next few days, that breeze would become a strong northerly wind, traditionally known here as *los vientos de octubre*, the winds of October.

He took her hand as they walked in silence along the bustling street. When a friend of Raúl's appeared and stopped to chat with him, a distracted Aída continued on towards the café. She was thinking about her father's words: he'd forbidden her to marry Raúl. You're too young, he had said; think of your future, finish school. She felt what might have been a twitch in her womb . . . she still hadn't told her father. Raúl had promised her he'd be back in a few months after the political situation cooled down. But when she tried to visualize a life together with Raúl and the baby, she saw only her father's scowling face.

The streets were crowded with midday traffic, noisy with horns and vendors' cries, when Aída's thoughts led her to turn around and look at

Raúl, who at that very moment was turning towards her. His receding hairline (just a boy, but so old! she thought) . . . Her schoolgirlish dress (she'll need new clothes soon, he fretted) . . . He gave her a quizzical look. A sad smile came to her lips.

Grandfather was fiddling with the shortwave radio, trying to tune in the guerrilla station. Nothing but static. With trembling hands, he began to slice the papaya he'd snipped from the tree in the backyard. He looked at his watch. In a few moments, he would switch on the TV for the midday newscast.

How many dead would there be today? he asked himself. And what would that communist of a president have to say about it? He held a slice of papaya up to his mouth and paused. He felt the cough begin deep inside his chest and he closed his eyes. The moist, pink fruit fell to the floor.

Grandmother was outside, watering the rose bushes next to the car-port when she heard him gasping for breath. Her jaw muscles were involuntarily taut, the effect of the speed-laced drug she'd been taking for her Alzheimer's condition. She stood motionless through grandfather's coughing fit, the water spouting from the hose and forming a muddy puddle under one of the rose bushes.

They had celebrated their fiftieth wedding anniversary the previous year. Shortly thereafter, his radiation treatments were suspended, and the cancer was declared inoperable. The house was filled with the aroma of the eucalyptus leaves that grandmother boiled for soothing teas day and night.

My family's home is in the hills above San Salvador, in an area known as Los Planes. The middle-class homes like my family's are on the hilltops. The poor live below, in the *barrancas*, on the sides of the steep valleys. The neighborhood was very quiet a few minutes before noon, except for the cough that my grandmother heard and that she could do nothing about.

Joaquín boarded the crowded, smoke-belching bus in front of the National University. He'd been checking out the possibility of a job there but, as they'd told him countless times before, the budget didn't allow for any new research positions in the Letters department.

He'd been bouncing from one low-paying job to another. The money was always running out, but he kept on writing. He'd often told me that he'd had it with this capital city whose name means "The Savior" yet which seems so far from being saved; but as a writer, he felt the responsibility of staying on and bearing witness to the history of his country, which he'd nicknamed *un monstruo de espinas*, his "spiny little monster." He was still Catholic enough to believe, as he would tell friends at literary drinking sessions, that "all this pain, all this suffering has got to be for something."

But he was finding it harder and harder to keep the faith. Maybe it wasn't such a bad idea to spend a few months in Mexico or the States. Or to retreat up to La Libertad province, to those hills that overlooked one of the few regions of nearly virgin jungle left in the country—during the day cultivate a little of the family's land, at night listen to his gregarious genius of an uncle rattle off biblical history . . . He was surrounded by the noise of the unmuffled buses, the obnoxious horns of the taxis, the trucks full of *guardias* with M-16s toted high, and the dust that poured in from the streets, gathering on his tattered penny loafers. He gazed through the open doorway at the harried pedestrians and counted the potholes that rattled the windows of the bus.

There had been few clients at the doctor's office that morning, so Patricia had been reading a romance novel, but she was finding it increasingly difficult to concentrate. She put the book down, reached into her purse and pulled out a small makeup mirror, teased her thick curly hair just a bit more. The reflection of the midday glare pouring through the third-floor office's windows caught her attention, and she turned around in her chair to gaze out at the ample view of the city and mountains beyond.

What would she do now? she asked herself. The man she had fallen in love with had left a few days ago and was now 3,000 miles away . . . she doubted that he would ever return. And earlier that day in a brief, troubling phone conversation, one of her close friends had told her that he was leaving for Mexico—perhaps for good. Maybe she would go back to school and study international relations, what she'd always wanted to do. But that would mean disobeying her mother. "Why do you want to study something so political? You'll just get into trouble." Her mother was thinking of the young men and women from their neighborhood who were involved in *la política*. Many of them were friends since childhood. Some were now in the mountains. Some in exile. Others, dead.

She stared at Guazapa, the mountain that dominated the city's northern skyline and that resembled a heap of molten obsidian. It was only a few kilometers from Apopa, her home town. When the bombs fell on the guerrilla strongholds on Guazapa, she could feel the walls of her family's home shudder.

She snapped the mirror shut and looked at her watch: 11:48. She got up, adjusted her bright, striped dress and started for the door. She would be lunching alone again, she thought, as she reached for the doorknob.

Raúl's grin answered Aída's . . . Grandfather was wiping tears from his eyes . . . Grandmother finally moved on to another rose bush . . . Joaquín visualized an ex-girlfriend . . . Patricia was opening the door . . . At exactly 11:49, they all heard what they thought was the familiar sound of a bomb exploding in the distance. The only difference was, it seemed to be coming from all directions at once, even from beneath one's feet.

My God, here, downtown? thought Patricia. Why here—can't they just keep their war away, far away? But no, it couldn't be . . . the shaking was going on too long. She hurried back into the office. The building swayed and moaned. She watched the typewriter inching towards the edge of the desk. She reached for it, but it went over: crash and ring. She sensed a shadow over her: the file cabinet. She moved out of the way and watched it fall . . . like slow motion. The walls cracked and plaster fell. Patricia frantically shook the dust from her hair.

"*¡Puta!*" Joaquín cursed out loud, when he felt the bus lurch violently. These streets get worse every day! Then he noticed the driver struggling with a steering wheel that had taken on a mind of its own. The brakes squealed, and Joaquín instinctively jumped through the door onto the street. He looked up and saw a church steeple rocking back and forth, the hands of the clock stuck on 11:50. Why would the bells be ringing at that hour? he wondered. He saw a grey-haired priest rush down the steps, hands crossed over his head: Like a prisoner. Then he saw an older, woodframe building collapse and a cloud of dust explode upwards. It was just like his family's home in San Esteban, about a mile from where he stood. As soon as the shaking stopped, he started running in that direction.

Grandfather watched the tables and chairs "dance a *cumbia*" in the living room. Grandmother, still outside, couldn't move because of the intensity of the shaking, so she lay down flat on her stomach, watching the concrete of the patio roll like waves on the ocean and fissure into a jagged puzzle. She cried out to her husband. The house shuddered so violently that she was sure it would fall. Grandfather struggled to open the door, but it was jammed. It would take all his strength, along with my grandmother's, to open it.

Raúl looked up and saw huge cracks split the walls of the library, as all the downtown buildings joined in the furious dance. Aída was a few yards ahead of him when the initial jolt caused her to tumble onto the sidewalk. Raúl, struggling to stay on his feet, ran and reached her, pulling her into the middle of the street to avoid the debris falling down around them. Embracing, they watched dozens pour out panic-stricken from the office buildings.

The quake was over in a matter of seconds. Then a dead silence. Then, in crescendo: screams, the squeal of tires, sirens, dogs howling. Vehicles and pedestrians charged to and fro. Raúl watched as an evangelist began shouting a spontaneous sermon atop a heap of dusty rubble: "*¡Esto es la voluntad de Dios!*" This is the will of God!

A thick cloud of dust rose up and hung over the city.

I was sitting at my desk in Los Angeles, going over notes for an article about my recent trip to El Salvador, a two-month stay that had ended five days before.

The news came to me as tragic news often does, with a voice over the phone saying, "Look, don't get too upset about what I'm going to tell you . . ." At the sound of four banal syllables, "seven-point-five," I found myself making two movements at once—the hand that held the receiver started to hang up, while the rest of my body turned suddenly, as if headed for the door. I froze. The thought of the distance paralyzed me.

A few minutes later, the voice on the other end of the line was that of a clerk at the airport. I made a reservation on the next available flight out.

The taxi winds up the road that leads to my family's home in Los Planes. Hundreds of makeshift shacks have been erected overnight on hillsides that were barren before. People walk alongside the road hauling salvaged belongings; others are sitting in front of damaged or destroyed homes, dazed looks on their faces.

I walk the final kilometer to the house. Many of the high white walls that surround the middle-class homes are toppled. My steps quicken as I reach the gate of my family's property. The walls that surround it haven't fallen, but are all cracked, threatening to come down. The first thing I see as I walk through the gate is my grandfather, lying on a bed in the middle of the patio, underneath a bedsheet draped across the clotheslines. Grandmother is at his side.

"You wouldn't believe what we've been through," she says.

Grandfather is quiet. He leans over and turns on the radio, tuned to the only station that survived the quake. He lies back down, folds his hands over his chest, and listens to the damage reports. His eyes stare straight into the white of the sheet above him.

The Rubén Darío building was named after Nicaragua's famous modernist poet, but I'll always remember it for *El Caminante*, The Traveller, the fruit juice bar on the southeast corner of its first floor. At midday and after school, all the bright orange stools and booths were occupied by boisterous teens sipping on mango or papaya malts. I too frequented the *Caminante*, sitting alone to read the papers and watch the young girls flirt with their awkward, adolescent suitors.

To enter the Darío, one always had to push and shove across a sidewalk crowded with pedestrians, street vendors, shoeshiners and beggars. The vendors sold anything from pocket combs to cassettes of Creedence Clearwater Revival, while the beggars displayed deformed limbs, eyeless sockets.

Now there is no sign of any of the first-floor cafés or shops. Dozens of rescue workers clamber over the debris of the block-long, six-floor building that was twisted and broken by the quake into a two-story mausoleum. The fifty or so people inside the *Caminante* when the quake hit, along with over five hundred others who were in the legal, dental and business offices in the building's upper floors, were crushed to death or trapped inside the smoldering rubble. Many of the vendors and beggars were buried under the building's eaves.

Behind a cordon of soldiers across the street, the families of those trapped inside maintain a vigil. There is still a chance that there are survivors: faint murmurs have been heard now and then issuing up through the rubble.

The Darío had been slated for demolition after the 1965 earthquake. But intransigence on the part of the ownership led to a compromise with city engineers: the two top floors would be removed, thereby relieving the supporting columns of enough pressure to make it "earthquake safe." This latter order was never fulfilled either.

Someone shouts for silence, and the jackhammers and bulldozers go quiet. A group of rescue workers listens intently at an aperture in the rubble. The wind rises and office trash skitters along the street past the relatives who stand frozen, holding handkerchiefs to tearful eyes. After a long while, there is a shaking of heads. The work resumes.

I visit San Jacinto, a hard-hit working-class *barrio* southeast of downtown San Salvador. Up and down nearly every street, residents pick through the rubble of their destroyed homes. The majority of homes in San Jacinto, like in all poor *barrios* of San Salvador, were built with *bahareque*, a thin bamboo-like wood, and simple mud brick.

I come upon a group of men rolling a black upright piano down the middle of the street. Its owner is Manuel Araujo, known to everyone here as the "maestro." In his fifties, pepper-haired and diminutive, he answers questions readily, with a plaintive smile. "My house," he says, pointing to the ruins from which he and his friends have just extricated the piano. "I've lost everything, except the piano. It's a miracle," he says, running his hand over the shiny black finish. "Not a scratch."

I am given a grim tour of the destruction on the block. On the corner is a grammar school whose roof gave way, killing over thirty schoolgirls. Across the street is an orphanage where dozens more children were injured.

RUBÉN DARÍO BUILDING

San Salvador 1986

When we return to the piano, an older woman in a tattered dress takes Manuel by the arm and whispers to him. He nods quietly. Someone brings him a chair, and he sits down before the piano. The salvage work pauses, as Manuel's neighbors, young and old alike, gather around. Softly, beautifully, the melody of a Brahms sonata fills the *barrio*. The shadows of the afternoon have lengthened around us and the remaining light gilds the dust raised by the cool, steady breeze. There is quiet applause when Manuel finishes. The woman in the tattered dress embraces him tearfully.

After the modest concert, one of Manuel's friends beckons to me. René Aquino, like Manuel, appears emotionally spent, on the verge of tears or violence, but he offers his impressions readily, hungry to be heard.

"Look at those people walking by there," he says, pointing at a crew of journalists with videocams. "They're not from the neighborhood—they've only come to see us suffer. We've lost everything. My house," he says, his eyes filling with tears and his hands going up to cover his face. He reaches out to me and pulls me close to him. "Come back and visit me, please. I live—I mean, I lived—right over there, around the corner. Please come back, my dear friends, I love you, you know, I love my new friends . . ."

The third day after the earthquake, San Salvador awakens to skies swept clean by steady winds. The air is cool and dry. Summer has begun.

Though there is no phone service and traveling around the city remains difficult, I succeed in getting word to Raúl and Aída through friends, and we meet for the first time since the quake. We head for the National University, hoping that is where many of our friends will be.

Upon arriving, we join hundreds of students standing on the lawns before the badly damaged buildings. Among them is Joaquín, my writer friend. After his mad dash from downtown, he'd found his family's house still standing—minus half a wall that tumbled down in the living room. "My family was all right," he tells me. "But I couldn't believe it, that is, I didn't believe them. I kept asking them if they were okay." He was in the living room when the first aftershock hit. "The shaking began, and I felt my body leap out through the hole in the wall. The roof caved in right on the spot where I'd been standing."

"Spiny, shitty little monster of a country," Joaquín curses. He asks me if I have any marijuana. I don't—we settle for making a date for a beer session. "I'm beginning to think that the suffering here only leads to more suffering. There's no Savior for the City of the Savior." Joaquín giggles, and I give him a confused look. "Didn't you hear about the Savior of the World?" he asks me, in reference to the city's famous statue of Christ, a tall pylon topped by a blue-green globe upon which a gleaming white Savior stands. "He fell over in the quake. Fell face flat onto the street and broke into a thousand pieces!" He giggles again. "And the statue of Christopher Columbus, the one in front of the National Palace? His head fell off!" The absurd images lead us to a fit of uncontrollable laughter. Then the wind rises again, and I feel a shiver.

I join Aída and Raúl, who are organizing rescue brigades that will concentrate their efforts in the *barrios* most affected by the quake. When we have a chance to speak alone, I ask Raúl about his political—and love—situation.

"The earthquake hasn't changed things," he says. "The death squads could take advantage of the chaos to disappear more people. But death threat or no death threat, this is where I'm needed. As soon as things are back to normal, I know I have to go. And Aída . . . I don't know. I don't want to take her to Mexico City. We'd be living practically on the streets. But leaving her behind . . . I just don't know."

I join a rescue brigade of students from the university. We flag down a pickup for a ride to the Santa Anita *barrio*. The minute we jump off the truck, the group is accosted by dozens of residents. All at once, they call out their symptoms, pleading for relief.

"Do you have something for nerves? I haven't slept in days," says an older woman with trembling hands.

A man says, "I've got a terrible headache, whatever you have, I'll take it."

"I have a terrible pain here," a woman says, both hands behind her back over her kidneys.

Makeshift tents line the streets. Most of the homes in Santa Anita were made of *bahareque*. All the residents, from tots to grandparents, are salvaging what they can—mangled dolls, unbroken dishes. All are covered with a layer of dirt from working in the dusty wreckage of what once were their homes. I find myself coughing and spitting up dirty phlegm.

We dispense our limited supplies quickly. All we have are aspirin, cough mixture for the children who've caught colds from sleeping outside at night, and the most basic first-aid supplies. In the morning, we heard the radio report that the country's drug supply was exhausted.

Near midday a government truck wheels into the neighborhood with meals for the homeless. Tortillas with beans and salt—not much different from the usual diet in the *barrios*. A small boy comes to me and insists that I eat. He introduces himself as Quique and says he is six years old. I ask him about his house. "Gone." His school? "Gone." Then he offers a curious observation. "There's a dog in the neighborhood that was run over by a truck this morning. The tire ran right over his neck. But he's still alive," he says, emphasizing the miracle of the dog's survival. When I get up to leave, Quique asks me to take his picture. Usually, young children who do so clown around before the camera, but not Quique. He stares intently at me while I focus. "Alive," I say to myself, as the shutter snaps.

The university's rescue brigades set up a command post at Cuscatlán Park, not far from the military hospital, where soldiers missing one or another limb are a common sight. I am surprised one afternoon to find my girlfriend Patricia, whom I've been able to visit only briefly since my arrival, at the university post, helping Raúl and Aída to organize requests for more supplies.

The doctor's office where she works as a secretary has been closed since the quake. A few nights ago, she organized several friends in her home town and they stayed up until the dawn, cooking meals for the homeless in the *barrios*. "Maybe it was enough for a hundred families. Next to nothing."

I try to reassure her that every effort counts, but find myself feeling much like her; I've been giving aspirin to people who have lost everything.

"What's taken the war seven years," Patricia observes, "was equalled in eight seconds of shaking."

A couple of days later, I again stand before the Darío building. After several days of continuous rescue work, it is perhaps only one-third of the mass of rubble I had seen upon my arrival. The scent of death rises from the ruins. Like everyone else, I hold a handkerchief over my mouth and nose.

A group of yellow-suited Mexican rescue workers search through the remains of the building. *Topos* they are called, moles. After the Mexico City quake of 1985, these wiry men burrowed through narrow passages in the collapsed buildings and saved dozens of people trapped inside, some of whom had survived longer than a week without food or water. The Mexican team made a highly visible trip to San Salvador soon after the quake. The TV lights followed their every movement.

But so far the *topos* have uncovered only corpses, and the hope for survivors is by now next to nothing. The TV cameras are gone. The Mexican disaster, at least, offered the collective redemption of dramatic rescues. No such miracles for El Salvador.

But the families of the dozens still trapped inside maintain their vigil day and night. I stand with a small group of print journalists, watching the rescue workers remove more rubble. At one point, all of them gather around one spot, where a crane lifts a huge chunk of concrete. Another body has been discovered.

The journalists begin jockeying for position as the body is lowered down to street level. The rescue workers call out for the relatives of a Dr Pineda. Several soldiers on watch nearby form a cordon around the body, trying to keep back the journalists. But it is apparent that the soldiers, like everyone else, are concerned with getting their own good look.

It resembles a bundle of spent firewood . . . he wore Oxford shoes . . . there is his name tag, half melted, stuck to the black tatters of his white smock.

The relatives arrive. They give a quick, tearless look. They nod at the rescue workers, then walk away, trying to avoid the press.

I am drafted, along with a university brigade, to assist the Comité de Señoras Pro Obras Sociales, the Wives' Committee on Social Projects. The organization is run by the First Lady of El Salvador, Inez Duarte.

The offices of the Comité are located in the Escalón neighborhood, the upper-class oasis a couple of miles from downtown San Salvador. Predictably, the Escalón, where the mansions are surrounded by tall walls topped with shards of glass imbedded in concrete, and by sentinels armed with M-16s, is one of the areas least affected by the quake. There isn't the slightest sign of a crack on the walls or streets.

We spend hours packing small bags of beans, rice, flour and milk, along with random scraps of children's clothing, into sacks. They will be donated one sack per family in the *barrios*, each enough to supply a family of five for two days.

The walls of the Comité's office are lined with photographs. All are variations on one theme: the First Lady among the poor. In some, the rather pale and plump Señora Duarte towers above them on steps or stages, standing next to religious and military officials. In others, she is amidst the masses, personally handing over donations to dark-skinned *campesinos* with gaunt faces, sunken eyes, bony hands.

The plastic used to wrap the foodstuffs is extremely thin. Bags of flour and dried milk keep bursting on me, the white powder falling on the marble floor of the Comité's office.

Almost one week after the quake, late afternoon: Raúl, Aída, and dozens of students are resting at Cuscatlán Park after another day of relief work. In the downtown area and in the *barrios*, thousands of tons of rubble have been removed, thousands of injured have been tended to. For the first time since the quake, the tension is lessening. We can feel it on the streets: the sirens don't wail as often, no longer is the traffic punctuated by desperate horns and curses.

I ask Raúl how long he thinks he will have to stay in exile. He has already spent two years in Mexico in the early 1980s because of earlier death threats.

"Another couple of years," he says. Then a smile comes to his lips. "Or maybe a year. Perhaps six months. Don't worry. I'm coming back. We're all going to come back."

Aída remains quiet and pensive, but through my mind run her words from an earlier time. Before leaving San Salvador on my previous trip, I had asked her to tape a message for Salvadoran refugees in Mexico and Los Angeles. She had obliged.

"Daily our people die," she had said, "because they don't receive enough love, because they don't have homes. Today, there are more *desplazados* [refugees] than yesterday, and tomorrow there will be even more . . . but every morning our people rise. Every dawn, the eyes of our people look towards the sun."

Aída dreams—as Raúl dreams, as has most of an entire generation of young Salvadorans dreamt since the late 1970s, of the birth of *la nueva patria*. Nearly a hundred thousand people, most of them in their teens and twenties, have paid the ultimate price for the realization of that dream. Only a few months ago, during excursions with Aída and Raúl into the countryside to visit politically organized groups of *campesinos*, I believed that dream as fervently as they did. But since the earthquake, I've found myself having doubts. About their young love, about my own relationship with Patricia, even about the revolution. The FMLN leadership has been telling us year after year that the *victoria final* was at hand, but today victory seems even further away than it did at the beginning of the war. I cannot voice my apprehensions. The response would be the rhetoric of *sacrificio*, the standard line about the "painful birth" of *la nueva patria*. A sense of dread grows within me; has *la nueva patria* been shattered by the shaking? Or had the dream already collapsed before the quake, without our having noticed?

After I say goodbye to Raúl and Aída, I leave them sitting on the curb quietly staring at the traffic rolling past: pickup trucks crowded with rescue workers, truckloads of soldiers, buses and taxis. Nearby them stands a *guardia*, on watch before the military hospital, hands resting on his M-16.

"All the fish leapt up out of the lake at once." Grandfather briefly sketches out the dramatic story of the eruption of the San Salvador volcano, which he witnessed as a young man in 1917. He falls silent, trying to catch his breath. His mouth opens and closes rapidly, as if he were biting at the air.

He has been talking lately of coming up to Los Angeles, "for a vacation." There is nowhere else for him to go now. Long gone are the days of trips to *el campo*, the rural areas, because they are now *zonas conflictivas*, the war zones. Gone too is the virgin tropical jungle he saw as a young man working on the railroad. Even Guazapa, his birthplace, has been bombed mercilessly and is sown with land mines. "The communists have ruined everything," he says. But even now, with all the destruction of the earthquake and the war, he still talks of a "vacation," not a permanent stay. He must spend his final days in the country of his birth.

Because of our radically different political points of view, our conversations have been reduced to superficial pleasantries. He knows he can't convince me. I know I can't change his entire lifetime's way of thought. I find myself thinking, we both want paradise. For El Salvador to return to the pre-war idyll of the tourist slogans: "El Salvador, the Land of Smiles." But no. That wasn't real . . . or was it? I believed every one of Grandfather's words when I was younger—even about how General Maximiliano Martínez had to get rid of the communists for the sake of the Fatherland. Grandfather's reactionary paradise, my socialist one . . . both impossible now. Death surrounds both our dreams: the war, the earthquake, his cancer. When I leave the house for the trip back to Los Angeles, we will embrace each other wordlessly.

I visit Joaquín in San Esteban. The house where his family now lives—untouched in the earthquake—is directly across the street from the pile of rubble that was once their home. It was morbid luck, this new house. The former owner, an older gentleman, had left for the western city of Santa Ana on the day of the quake. He died a day later, victim of a heart attack.

Joaquín and I walk the neighborhood, stopping before a collapsed two-story building. Across one wall, there had been a large red Coca-Cola sign. Now there is a jumble of letters: a fragment of *O*, a bit of *A*. A family of four died here, Joaquín tells me—a mother and her young children. "She managed to get the children together, but they didn't make it out. Only when the rescue teams came with heavy machinery could we free their bodies. When we did, we had to pry the children out of her arms."

We walk down one of the brothel-lined streets of the *barrio*. To our surprise, the prostitutes are doing business, even amidst the rubble of the collapsed buildings, sheets draped over the collapsed walls and candles burning instead of light bulbs. "Come on boys, get yours before the end of the world!" calls out a young woman, and the forlorn men that mill about on the street laugh. From inside one of the ruined buildings, we hear a bottle shatter.

"This hasn't always been a *zona roja* [red-light zone]," Joaquín tells me. "In the battle for independence, this *barrio* was one of the first to rise up in the rebellion."

But there are few signs of rebellion in San Esteban today. The headquarters of the Treasury Police—a medieval-looking fortress with gun turrets—is only a few blocks away. As Joaquín reminds me, they are just as involved as the National Police, the National Guard and the army in the kidnappings, torture and murders of those suspected of "subversion." "And, of course," he adds matter-of-factly, "I'm a suspected subversive."

"Raúl is gone," says Patricia when we meet on Sunday, ten days after the quake. "And so is Aída." One of the Mexican rescue teams on its way back home had offered them a free ride. The thought of not seeing either of them again leaves us silent for a long while. I think back to the last time I saw them, in the park. Raúl had said nothing about leaving so soon—or about their decision to leave together. I am happy for them, but the only image I can conjure of their new life is of them walking without direction on the streets of Mexico City, another city destroyed by shaking and a year later still trying to get back on its feet.

Patricia and I walk through the *barrios* without a destination. "We've lost everything," we hear again and again, and the scene is always the same: makeshift tents on the street, *bahareque* strewn about like toothpicks, dust swirling in the winds.

This time it is the Candelaria *barrio*, and it is Imelda, a 29-year-old marketwoman who speaks. Since the earthquake she hasn't gone to work, afraid to leave her children alone. "It's still shaking," she says. Indeed, everyone is wondering why the aftershocks haven't subsided. There is a persistent rumor that another large quake is on the way.

Further down the block we encounter a group of young people standing just inside the doorway of a small house. They call out to us—aren't we going to talk to them?

What do they think of the situation?

"*Jodídos, pero vivos.*" Fucked, but we're alive.

Later that day, I walk Patricia to the bus stop where she will catch a ride back to her family's home. The light of day fades and the headlights of the vehicles cut diagonals of light through the dusty darkness.

We had fallen in love a month before the quake, which wound up reuniting us much sooner than we had planned. We'd spent only a few hours together since then, meeting in one of the few cafés still standing downtown, or sitting on curbsides, holding each other before a backdrop of cracked walls and heavy traffic.

As we wait for her bus, she tells me she has decided to register at the university. "I don't care what my family says. I can't go on working in that office and just watch what's happening to the country, not being able to do anything about it." She speaks with the kind of conviction I've been used to hearing from Raúl and Aída. There is a seriousness to her demeanor that I've never seen before.

Perhaps not all is death, I think to myself. Patricia is willing herself toward the future, in spite of the war and the quake: she is growing up. In that same instant, I realize that our destinies will separate us. She seems to know where she's going. But me?

We say goodbye, and she boards her bus. I begin walking to my bus stop to catch a ride to my family's home. It suddenly strikes me as strange—amazing, even—that we have homes to go to, that we can catch rides and arrive at them.

On my last day in San Salvador, I visit the *barrios* one last time. Jorge, a photographer friend, accompanies me. He suggests that we head for one of the hard-hit hillside communities west of downtown, most of which bear the names of saints: San Jacinto, Santa Marta, Santa Carlotta. "The saints always suffer more," says Jorge, with typically dark Salvadoran humor.

In Santa Carlotta we arrive at the scene of a weary reconstruction effort. Several families are relocating their homes on empty lots adjacent to the *barrio*. Men clear brush with machetes and shovel away dirt to lay foundations. The women and children help as they can.

In Santa Marta, however, there is still an aura of death. Nearly forty families were given up for dead here when a mudslide crashed down on their shacks at the bottom of a *barranca*. The first time I visited Santa Marta, dozens of men were struggling to reach the bodies of the women and children buried underneath tons of mud and debris. The men complained that there was no help from the soldiers or the government. They needed heavy machinery to reach their loved ones. Finally a bulldozer did arrive, but it pulled out again for another disaster area before all the bodies had been recovered.

SALVAGE WORK
San Salvador 1986

The only people left working the site now are the relatives of three families still trapped below. "We're doing this ourselves, without any help from anybody," says an older man on the scene. His wife and two children are below. The mid-morning sun beats down on the bare backs of the men working in the soft, heavy mud.

Sightseers ask the old man why they haven't gone to ask for help. He maintains a weary patience as he answers that they have, that it's come and gone already. "Now, it's just us."

There are several soldiers on the scene, as at every other disaster area. And, as at every other death scene, they stand with their rifles and silence, guarding God knows what, watching the poor unearth their loved ones.

> *After an earthquake*
> *the walls of my* barrio
> *show more of their hunger and death . . .*

"It's a poem I wrote before all this happened," says Joaquín when I see him the night before my departure. He jokes about the premonitory powers of the poet.

I ask him if he is still planning to leave the country, as he had told me before the quake.

"Not right now. Maybe in the future . . . it wouldn't be for very long. But it's difficult to live here. This country's a spiny monster," he says, grimacing then smiling. "You've got to have balls to stand it."

> *Yesterday*
> *before they had invaded us*
> *with electronic*
> *dances and video games*
> *and there wasn't Martial Law*
> *nor state of siege*
> *nor earthquakes . . .*

Joaquín pulls some "subversive" books down from the shelf: Neruda, Hikmet, Dalton, Brecht. "But remember," he tells me in between swigs from a beer bottle. "All this pain has to be for something, for . . . *something*."

the children
would play ball
until midnight
because upon entering San Esteban
the moon
shone a different way.

Joaquín accompanies me to the bus stop for the last ride up to my family's home. We walk down the main street of *barrio* San Esteban. Night is falling. Everywhere we look are the soldiers, patrolling nervously. There's still no electricity here, so the street lamps aren't working, but a dim light guides us: it comes from the flames of the cooking fires that line both sides of the road in front of the destroyed homes. The countless fires, each one representing a family, remind me of the rows of candles that the faithful light in church before the statues of Jesus, the Virgin and the saints. The glow illuminates dimly the faces of the women leaning over steaming pots. The flames flicker in the breeze.

L.A. Journal (I)

April 1990

I am unpacking again. I am perpetually living out of boxes—boxes that are only half emptied before they must be filled and sealed again for the next move. But I want this stay to last a long time. I am in my late grandparents' house in the Silver Lake district of Los Angeles, in a hilly area of 1930s Deco homes that the Mexican side of my life has lived in for fifty years. The stay will not last long, though; I'm only caretaking the place for a few months while it's remodelled in anticipation of some yuppie's rent money.

In a couple of weeks Y will come up from Guatemala to stay with me for a month, so I pull out a few souvenirs and mementos from the boxes and hang them on the walls of my father's old bedroom so that there'll be a semblance of a home for us. I reach into a box and pick up a cardboard-framed photograph. "Baptism Souvenir," reads the badly printed cursive. "Our Lady Queen of the Angels (Old Mission Plaza)."

Nuestra Señora la Reina de Los Angeles de Porciúncula is the original, overwrought Catholic for the Old Plaza Church, which is popularly known as La Placita—the site of the city's founding. Every Sunday, thousands of Mexicanos, Chicanos and Centroamericanos come to hear one of the twelve masses offered at La Placita, dressed to kill in rented suits or humbly in home-stitched silk dresses. Around those who have come to baptize their kids swarm the photographers. Among these latter, on one Sunday in the fall of 1962, must have been one George A. Pérez, whose name is printed on the back of the cardboard frame.

Our Lady Queen of the Angels
(OLD MISSION PLAZA)

Baptism Souvenir

BAPTISM
La Placita 1962

The image is marred by rust-colored scratches, the result of a gloss-enhancing wash that was probably Sr Pérez's finishing touch; year by year, the acid eats away at more and more of the picture. Flanking the silver-haired priest (horn-rimmed glasses, lips pursed) is a well-dressed, elderly couple. His aquiline, Northern–Mexican nose gives him an air of dignified *mestizo*ness, leaning away from the Spaniard and towards the *indígena*; she, light complected, with large eyes, high cheekbones and a wide smile (less *indígena*). My Grandparents. The camera has captured the very moment when the priest lets the water drip onto the head of a smiling kid swathed in virgin white. Me.

It is just a few days before the October Missile Crisis. My grandparents' restaurant has taken shape on Glendale Boulevard. Elvis Presley stopped by not long ago (my grandparents had no idea who he was) and left a note behind: "Nice place, great food. Elvis Presley." The napkin he wrote on will become my younger sister's prize possession. My father is doing litho work at a place called Rapid Blue Print, making $1.50 an hour, good money for a first-generation Mexican. He likes to slick his hair back, but he is not a *pachuco*—he's proud to speak an unaccented English as well as a flawless Spanish. And, as he is still wont to say thirty years later, he is also proud to be better off than the *chusma*, the rabble, such as the recently arrived immigrants who gather in squalor in the *barrios* to the south and to the east of La Placita. My mother's doing her best at playing the classic housewife, watching a lot of TV (which inspires her to do her hair up like Jackie Kennedy's), singing nursery rhymes to me in Spanish, and probably still thinking a lot about her native El Salvador, which she left only a few years before. My parents live in their newly built house in Silver Lake (only five minutes away from my grandparents). It's all very middle-class idyllic and I'm the model first-born son. My parents often have representatives of the fledgling Latino middle class over to the house for martinis and cha-cha dancing, the men with Brylcreemed hair and sharp suits with thin ties, the women with knee-length polka-dotted dresses and their hair teased into Roman arches.

Father must work eighteen, sometimes twenty hours a day, and the loneliness begins to take its toll on my mother. Late one night, alone in the house, her son fast asleep, feeling the isolation, longing for the comfort of the large family she left behind in El Salvador—this, too, is exile—and awed by the vastness of a city she doesn't understand, she locks herself in the bathroom. My father finds her still there, shaken and wordless, in the early morning hours. From then on, I knew that there were monsters lurking outside in the darkness of the city, poised to leap and tear my family apart.

There's a War

And mothers and sons
and a cool night breeze.
The insects lean
on the houses,
curl around our fingers.
In our ears a
sledgehammer
pounds the mountain,
the insects land
on the face, the face
now broken lava, the lava
running down my mother's
cheek. I am twelve.
I hear machine guns downtown.
I am twenty-four. My grandfather
was born in Guazapa.
1909. Thirty thousand dead.
1932.
Today, insects on the highway,
inside the radios of
all the cars. On TV,
they live in the announcer's
throat. The news pours.
I must write.
I must love.

The witnesses crowd
around the body.
The body is now
one hundred thousand.
The year is one-thousand-
nine-hundred-eighty-six.
The numbers are called
by the insects.
We dance.
The floor is slippery.
It is hot red,
a volcano beneath our feet.
The night slap of
helicopter blades slits
backs, enters the sleep
of the mother.
There is nowhere to go.
I knew that
when I got here.
I knew about this.
But now the pounding
is twenty miles away,
on the mountain
where grandfather was born.
It calls to me, says:
Join me,
join me,
in the breaking
the interrogating,
in the slap, pound, stab,
finish the face with me . . .
Stand beneath me.
Let me crumble you
under the weight of class.

San Salvador, 13 August, 1986

Homecoming

San Salvador, December 1987

The shadow of the plane darts across dusty fields that give off pale smoke as they are burned before the sowing of winter's crops. Spontaneous combustion and lightning strikes are also common during the long dry season, and the brittle yellow remnants of the richly cultivated landscape catch fire easily. I can't help but imagine the blazes that rise up where rockets pound into the thickly forested hills along the Honduran border—beyond the cultivated plains, beyond the volcanos and valleys, somewhere beyond the horizon.

Yet another homecoming. My second home. My first home. My no-home . . . I pass through the lightly guarded customs area without a hitch—sometimes press credentials *can* help you in El Salvador. I had told my family not to bother to pick me up, but as the automatic doors that open onto the main lobby separate with a mechanical whoosh, I scan the expectant faces anyway. A part of me wishes to see my grandparents smiling widely, my nephews waving. But the eyes only glance at me, then they are straining to find the familiar face behind me as the doors slam shut.

Outside, I negotiate in vain for a cheap fare into town, and end up paying fifty *colones* ($10, an exorbitant fee here) to the driver of a mid-seventies Toyota. As we speed along the open highway, I find myself immediately looking for signs of the conflict. But of course there are none. We are very far from the war of bullets and helicopters.

My driver fidgets with the radio, tuning it to a Top Forty station that blares out the Miami Sound Machine. I gaze through the window. Men, women and children carry firewood, large baskets, water gourds alongside the road. There are some soldiers out on patrol, supposedly guarding the highway, but it's been so long since the guerrillas have been in this part of the country that the soldiers look bored, expecting anything but an ambush.

I tell the driver that I was last here just after the earthquake. It had left San Salvador looking like the bombed-out towns of the remote country-side. Any progress?

"It's gone to hell."

I wince and grab onto the dashboard as he weaves in and out of the slower traffic. The Virgin Mary swings from the rearview mirror like a circus acrobat.

"Don't worry," says my driver, noticing my discomfort. "We're all experts at this."

We reach the end of the highway. The colonies of shacks built after the earthquake are still perched precariously on the hillsides below the middle-class homes; the dust still swirls about with the summer winds. As we move into downtown San Salvador, I see streets twice as congested with vendors as before. Their stalls of fruits and vegetables, clothing and cigarettes are spreading ever further out from the Central Market. The city is rapidly becoming one huge, neurotic bazaar.

Every morning during the Christmas and New Year's holiday, my nephew, five years old, awakes at dawn, pulls out his toys and turns on the TV at top volume. The adults, still in bed, grind their teeth. The only other person up at that hour is the maid, Nora, who loves to play pop radio, also at top volume, as she readies breakfast. A *cumbia* rhythm and the sounds of dishes clattering in the kitchen accompany the roosters that crow outside, and the dubbed voices of the cartoon characters GI Joe and the Masters of the Universe reverberate throughout the house.

In the rebuilt cottage adjacent to my uncle's large, comfortable home, my grandparents sleep. Grandfather is still alive, slowly losing his bout with cancer. Grandmother has been wishing that she might die with him. How I'd like to speak with grandfather . . . about life and death and love and war. But he is even quieter now than he was when I was twelve and he occasionally broke his long silences to tell me his tall tales, and I can't seem to find the confidence to say what I must say.

I am the first of the grown-ups awake. Sleepily, I sip some coffee, look out through the bars across the windows at the peaceful greenery of the backyard. As I walk outside past my grandparents' silent cottage and take the cobblestone path towards the bus stop, I feel pangs of guilt: I'm going to betray my family by visiting my other family.

The last time I saw Pedro, about a year and a half ago, he was in exile in Mexico City and drunk, after more than a decade of sobriety. It was at a hotel in the Zócalo area downtown, a cavernous nineteenth-century palace with a skylight and a daunting interior patio. The Mexican authorities were using the building to house exiles from all over Latin America—everyone from shell-shocked FMLN combatants to anti-Castro Cubans. Pedro's drunken rants bounced off the thick cold walls and echoed throughout the building.

"This one's for the boys fighting the fascists in the mountains!" he toasts with the bottle of brandy. He passes me the bottle, then grabs it out of my hands to continue. "And this one's for the whores who suck the soldiers' cocks! This one's for us, the fucked-up poets whose petty bourgeois decadence is as tragic a story as the Crucifixion!" The bottle flies toward the mirror. Pedro looks at himself in a hundred shards, weeping.

I had originally met him at the National University in El Salvador—that "den of subversion" that succeeding governments have singled out for repression—where he led poetry workshops in the bullet-riddled extension building. In Pedro's case, there is no doubt that his sentiments fell into the "subversive" category, at least in the government's eyes: his poetry speaks of suffering and hope (*"The bloody rain soaks into the black earth/and yet, the sunflowers manage to rise . . ."*), and sometimes outright militancy (*"The sons of the Conquest/will reconquer the land of the sun . . ."*). After collaborating with the rebels and publishing protest poetry in one of the country's major dailies, he was arrested and detained by the security forces.

In Mexico, with his usual hushed cadences, which faded in and out like a weak signal on a shortwave radio, he'd told me about the hideous poetry of that night: the soldiers' boots pounding on the roof . . . rifle butts

FAMILY
San Salvador 1988

smashing the floorboards . . . his daughters crying . . . bookshelves toppled . . . his wife stoically silent before the lieutenant's questioning . . . the leaves swirling about the house in the helicopter wind . . . the cockroaches skittering over his body in the dank cell.

He'd been lucky. Influential university authorities pulled diplomatic strings to get him off with a relative wrist slap: exile. But in Mexico City, the separation from home and family had driven him to the edge of insanity. (I imagine the bottle in one hand, a cigarette in the other: *"This is the first drink I've had in ten years, compañeros . . ."*) So he threw caution to the wind and risked returning, although there were no guarantees for his or his family's safety.

And so here he is, back in San Salvador, asleep after another late-night drinking session with his bohemian buddies when I arrive. His wife greets me, offers me coffee, and we chat quietly about Pedro's return while he showers. Yes, she says, it's a relief to have him home. But the anxiety remains, and no, she doesn't think the war will end soon, but what can one do?

When Pedro enters the room, shirtless, eyes reddened like coals, black hair unruly, a smile emerges from his deeply lined face. With his voice a whisper, on the verge of unintelligibility, he fills me in on the events of the last year. In Mexico, things had gone from bad to worse, he says. The pain of exile, coupled with his excessive drinking, had gotten him into more and more trouble.

One night, exasperated at not being able to contact his wife and daughters by telephone, the pressure became unbearable. He went on a rampage, bursting into his comrades' rooms and tearing the receivers off the telephones, which he deposited, one by one, in his room. None of his friends had been able to control him. When the police arrived, he was seated crosslegged on the bed, holding his head in his hands, surrounded by the black receivers and their severed cords.

The cry "*¡Felicidades!*" rings out in all directions. It is New Year's Eve and the house is filling with guests. My grandfather, the center of attention, seems happy: it is the first time in many years that his grandchildren from the United States have come to spend the holidays with him.

As ever, he comments on the political situation, which to him appears worse every day. He traces the trouble back to the late seventies and President Carter's emphasis on human rights. "This allowed the communists to gain strength."

An aunt chimes in. "What we need right now," she says, "is someone who isn't afraid of using force to get us out of this mess." (An image of Major Roberto D'Aubuisson flashes in my mind: he raises the machete and whacks the watermelon in half before a crowd of silent *campesinos*. "That's how the Christian Democrats are—green on the outside, but red on the inside! Communists!")

With the "human rights" stipulations, grandfather continues, the war against the communists was checked. And just look at the country today. "Duarte is a socialist," he says. "And you know that between socialism and communism, there is only a very small step. And that's where this country is heading." Grandmother shudders. "This thing about communism scares me," she says. She's been complaining about my beard lately: "Looks too much like Che."

I say nothing, though I'd like to steer the conversation away from the politics, to hear once again grandfather's stories. The one about the huge *hacienda* my family once owned comes to mind . . . *"Lands that stretched out as far as the horizon."* But all the memories have been truncated by the war.

I look at grandfather's hands. I always marveled at them as a child—large and strong, capable of wielding a machete or pulling on a railroad brake. The hands retain some of their youthful strength, though they are now liver-spotted. But his forearms, his chest and the rest of his body have thinned. The *guayabera* hangs too loose over his sagging shoulders.

The family around him laughs, drinks, dances. Grandfather, his political speech over, gasps for breath.

"That hotel was full of phantoms—exiles from all over the world. I was one of the ghosts too," says Pedro, sipping a morning beer at a bar downtown. The waitress, a pretty young woman with a disquieting, distracted look, serves us *boquitas*—small chunks of cheese and pork. She returns to her post behind the counter, looking out over the empty tables.

This is Pedro's second homecoming. After his first return, it hadn't taken long to find out if he was welcome. He'd been in the country only a week when several armed security agents burst into his mother's house and asked for him by name. Fortunately, he wasn't there, but he went into hiding and left the country again shortly thereafter.

Six more months of exile had the same effect on him as his previous stint. He phoned his wife and told her that he'd do anything—stay inside, not visit any of his old communist friends, take not one sip of alcohol—anything to be home again. His wife relented, and during the summer school break, he "visited" El Salvador once again. "The idea was to stay two weeks, to test the waters," he says, tousling his hair with a shaky hand. "I'm still living that two weeks, six months later."

During the first few months, he rarely went out, resisting the temptation to visit his colleagues. He spent endless hours working on his poetry. But as time passed and no rifle butts smashed down the door in the middle of the night, he gained confidence, and gradually began venturing out onto the streets.

Still, it has been a bit much for me to take, to see him mentioned, lauded even, in the country's main right-wing paper by a columnist friend of his, who wrote a glowing commentary upon a new collection of poems by Pedro. He has also given a public reading at the Teatro Nacional, the plushly carpeted, chandeliered, government-run cultural center.

In effect, he is being toasted by the very government that two years ago kicked him out of the country, but Pedro reminds me that there still remain a couple of unknowns in the equation. Sure, there is more political space today—he probably wouldn't get busted for his poetic pamphlets now—but one could never trust the authorities that much . . . the fear is still there. And then there is the situation with his oldest daughter.

I give Pedro a querulous look.

"You haven't heard, I guess," he says, as he meticulously peels the label off the beer bottle. "Now we've got two troublemakers in the family. She's working full-time with a human rights organization. That could interest the authorities. Not just in her, but in my case again as well. It's a real family affair, now."

My uncle pours himself another vodka. It is still early in the evening, but my uncle Roger's New Year's "celebration" is more than well underway. We sit uncomfortably, next to each other, for a few minutes.

The years are most apparent in his balding pate, in his large belly and in not just the rings under his eyes but the eyes themselves: they look down, away from you—too tired to meet your gaze straight on. But ever the responsible father, even though he's in the process of going through his second divorce, Roger gets up each morning, goes to work to support his children. No hangover has ever stopped him.

Finally, we hit upon a subject that animates him: business. He works for a Japanese-owned textile factory on the outskirts of the city, one of the largest in the country and among the few that has managed to hold its own during the war. Now in his element, Roger warms up to what sounds like a speech he's given many times.

Yes, it surely was one of the largest in the Central American market. These last few years have been ones of adversity though, no doubt about it. Lay-offs. Rebel sabotage. And the time the Japanese Chief Executive Officer was kidnapped by the guerrillas. The FMLN asked for millions of dollars for his release. Endless negotiations for nothing: it all went awry in the end. Seems that an overzealous army commando unit attempted to ambush the guerrillas at the pre-appointed drop-off site. After the gun battle, the executive's bullet-riddled body was sent back home to Japan, and the ambassador asked for some military heads to roll. The FMLN, on the other hand, succeeded in getting the cash. An ex-guerrilla once told me about a mad shopping spree after the incident, eating out at expensive restaurants, hiring taxis even for short trips, renting out hotel rooms for romantic encounters. . . . *A crew of guerrillas disguised in white* guayaberas *at the Salvador Sheraton, wining and dining the daughters of the aristocracy* . . .

Roger's voice drifts back to me. The company's in a holding pattern these days, he says; no growth, no shrinkage. Everything stays the same. It's a depressing situation, you know?

He raises the glass to his lips, closing his eyes as he savors the drink. The ice cubes clink and some vodka spills over the rim as he sets the drink down too hard upon the glass table.

It is late in the afternoon at the National University, and I wait for Pedro's daughter, Soledad, to show up for our meeting. She is late, and I wonder about her new job, with the human rights organization.

The university is virtually unchanged: it lives up to its reputation as a "liberated zone," with FMLN recruitment propaganda blaring through speakers outside the Psychology building, along with Cuban New Song by Silvio Rodríguez and Pablo Milanes. And the graffiti—ever since I can remember, almost every wall here has been covered with spray-painted slogans. Some walls sport several generations of them, dating back to the sixties. Each year there is a new set of slogans, but the theme never changes. *Duarte, ¡A la mierda!* is this year's favorite—"Duarte, to the shits!"

There do seem to be more student organizations (each slogan is signed by one group or another), though. The most radical have taken to taunting the security forces by throwing rocks, obviously wanting them to fire into the crowd and further radicalize the masses. But there are other students who tell me they feel this tactic is infantile. And there are significant numbers on the sidelines, genuinely interested in social change but utterly confused as to who is representing which faction and who is right.

Soledad arrives at the very moment when I'd given the date up for lost. She has many of her father's features: a prominent but pretty mole to the left of her nose, a mischievous smile, dark and radiant eyes.

"I'm not sure what to do," she tells me, as we sit down for coffee at an open-air campus café packed with students. The job with the organization has caused somewhat of a crisis in the family, she admits.

It was almost by chance that Soledad happened into the job. Only a few months ago, she had abandoned hope of finishing her studies in the unpredictable and dangerous environment of this university, where her father's notoriety (the poetry workshops) cast a peculiar shadow upon her. Last year she had visited a friend who was studying at Mexico City's finest university, and she began to consider completing school there instead, an idea her parents loathed. A short while later, however, she was offered the job and, she says, "Everything changed."

"I've been learning so much." Soledad flashes a smile. "I work a lot directly with the *campesinos*, and I've never had that experience before."

Again, her parents had objected—especially Pedro: *"What about school? You'll never be able to finish your studies with a full-time job! You know that we love you, but you have to understand my political situation, dear . . ."*

"Now, my parents say they want me to go to Mexico," Soledad says, smiling only slightly at the irony. She averts her gaze from me, out towards the gathering darkness. There are fewer students now and the waitresses are preparing to close down the café.

I find myself somewhat surprised that Soledad has gone so wholeheartedly into the political movement. When we first met, she had given me the impression that activism wasn't one of her ambitions. "I know what I'm doing," she stresses. "And to me, all politics is a dirty business. But there are some pure things. Like helping the *campesinos*. They're not ideologues. So I feel like I'm doing some good. At least . . . I'm not on the other side."

I step outside into the cool night air, under the canopy of the giant copinol tree in the backyard. Across the valley, roman candles toss rainbow colors into the air. Steadily, the sound of fireworks going off in the hills around us and in the city below has been increasing. An hour before midnight, we begin raising our voices to be heard over the multitudinous explosions.

"This is nothing," says Pablo, another one of my uncles, with his ironic smile, just a few minutes before midnight. "Back when people still had money, you could hear twice as much on New Year's." As with my uncle Roger, the economy is one of Pablo's favorite topics. He asks me about the Black Monday stock market crash in the States. "What in the hell is going on over there? How is it that your economy could seem so strong and then in one day, *pffft!*?"

Pablo has been dancing *cumbias* tirelessly, and everything he says is tinged with irony, but now it seems as if he's truly asking me to explain what went wrong with supply-side economics. "We haven't begun to feel it here yet. But we will," he says gravely.

Pablo goes on to relate an anecdote which, he says, will show just how bad things are in El Salvador now. He was walking downtown just the other day, in broad daylight, when an assailant tore a thick gold chain from his neck. "Six hundred dollars lost." But it's okay, he tells me. "Right afterwards, I bought myself this." He thrusts up his arm, fist clenched, to show me his new gold bracelet. "Two hundred dollars."

The full fury of the fireworks is let loose at the stroke of midnight. All the sounds of the war are reproduced in the celebratory din. Strings of firecrackers imitate machine guns. Large, dynamite stick lookalikes boom out like mortar cannons. From dozens of different points around the city, skyrockets streak across the sky. There are so many detonations that the individual blasts become one solid hail of noise. It is that sound I will remember most: when I think back later and try to remember what people said in those moments, I will see the lips forming words, but there will be no sound other than explosions.

Later, the family gathers together in the living room for a toast to begin the New Year. Pablo is visibly drunk, but suddenly eloquent.

"We propose this toast, in honor of the entire family. But this toast, more than anything else, is a tribute to this couple," he says, motioning towards my grandparents, "who, through their example of longevity and loyalty, inspire all of us . . ."

The glasses clink all around the room. My grandfather, fatigued (he has already had to lie down once this evening to catch his breath), manages a smile.

Both Soledad and I shiver. Night has fallen upon the campus, and the cool breeze of the afternoon has given way to a stiff evening wind.

A small black monkey hops from table to empty table, vainly looking for scraps of food. Soledad is steeped in her thoughts. In a few moments, both the waitresses and monkey are gone.

Soledad knows she can't take the argument about her family's safety lightly. She recently attended the funeral of Herbert Anaya Sanabria, the slain leader of another human rights organization identified with the Left. The death squads have been coming out of hiding lately, and as well as Sanabria's murder, there have been dozens of less-publicized "disappearances" of students and labor leaders.

Should she go to Mexico, as her family wants her to do, as she herself had felt was perfect only months ago? Stay on, working with the *campesinos*? Quit, but stay in El Salvador and study at the university?

"The thing is, I don't want to miss any of this history," she says, as a gust of wind plays with her thick curly hair (which is just like her father's). "Though I know there's more to the world than just El Salvador, and there's so much to see in Mexico City."

One thing is for certain: she can't continue at odds with her father. "When I was younger, he would play me his favorite music and read his poetry." She smiles at the memory. "But I didn't understand. I rejected him. And when he left the country, I . . ." She pauses, and her eyes, focused on the empty space between us, appear to conjure up his image again, and I see him too: *in the living room, reciting from a book before his bohemian friends . . . passed out in his study, his head resting over a furiously edited manuscript . . .* "I realized that the things he was trying to share with me were really beautiful. Those things began to mean so much to me while he was gone. And now that he's back . . . it's like he's not really here. Do you think he's really in danger?"

The full moon is rising above the horizon and as we get up to leave, the buildings of the university are silhouetted against the pale light. We walk into the darkness outside the glow of the café's lights.

"What would you do?" she asks.

Pedro and I are sharing a joint out on the patio. His youngest daughter, a cute four-year-old, bounds out to greet him, her black hair shiny and wet from a bath. The day is bright, the sun strong and warm. As the grass takes effect and my body relaxes, I gaze out at the neighborhood. Just a few blocks away is the National University. Pedro hasn't set foot on the campus in over two years, and he continues to resist the temptation to do so. Two blocks down in the opposite direction stands an army barracks.

I notice a dark band on the eastern horizon. Smoke? I ask Pedro. He peers at the phenomenon and shrugs his shoulders. "I've got my escape route all worked out," he jokes. "I hear them at the door, I jump over this wall and I'm gone," he says, nodding his head at the five-foot wall that surrounds the narrow patio. Suddenly, as if on cue, we hear the sound of the doorbell. "There they are now," he says.

Agents in civilian clothes throw us against the wall for the body search. One of them is shouting obscenities, asking where the weapons are stashed. The bookshelves, Neruda, Vallejo ("¡Comunistas!" yells a soldier), tumble to the floor. Pedro's youngest daughter is screaming and his wife is trying to calm her down. One soldier is prodding Soledad with his rifle, telling her how "good she looks." And now they are asking what the hell an American journalist—a suspiciously Salvadoran-looking American journalist—is doing in the house of a "known Communist terrorist." What am I going to tell my family? Then we're thrown into one of those red Cherokee jeeps with tinted windows. After a long ride, we are ordered out in the middle of nowhere. In an abandoned ranch house, the shots ring out . . .

"The risk is very real," says Pedro, snapping me out of the vision, and he passes me the joint. Back inside the house, he confides that his stay here feels "like a temporary one." He puts a shirt on, finishes off a cup of coffee and searches for his cigarettes. Then he thinks out loud, muttering in fragments, "Maybe the best thing . . . Mexico again . . . fucking fascists . . ." (Later, when I ask his wife if she'll join him in exile should he leave again, she gives me a tired shake of the head. Will this moving never stop?)

As we are about to leave, Pedro's youngest daughter bounds into the living room. "Where are you going, daddy?" she asks, stretching her arms out to him for a goodbye hug and kiss on the cheek.

"I'm just going downtown for a little while, my love." After embracing her, Pedro turns toward me again. For a few moments, he gives me a wordless, troubled look, then we walk through the door and out onto the city streets.

In the rattling bus, on our way to different destinations (Pedro to check on the printing of his new book, I towards home for lunch with my family), Pedro invites me to spend New Year's Eve with him. "I'll show you what a real New Year's Eve celebration is like here," he tells me . . . *Communist Party veterans and young radicals from the university dancing up a sweat, booze and grass, Soledad and me stealing a kiss in the backyard . . .* I can't, I tell Pedro, I have to spend time with my family.

The fireworks have begun to taper off, the battle sounds more distant. Outside on the patio, Roger sits before me, and between us is the bottle. A floodlight shines from the house behind him; his face is in perfect silhouette. "Look. I'll tell you something," he says, his mouth dry from the alcohol. "Some friends have approached me in the past and have said, 'Come on, let's join in the fight against the guerrillas.' But I told them no.

"There are many different ways of fighting. . . . I think the most important one is economic development. They have to let the middle class have a chance to right things." But he's too drunk to maintain his train of thought. Soon he's talking about the family.

Things never seem to turn out the way you dreamed they would, he says. Yes, the second divorce has been tough, but his kids still love him—nothing can break that bond. "Look. I'll tell you what's really the most important thing, more important than my money and your words and all that shit. Family, that's what." He appears to be on the verge of tears, but he holds it in. Then a sneer flashes across his face. "The fucking *gringos* don't know anything about family, and, unfortunately for you, you grew up with them.

"Without the family, we don't have anything. Because of business, I've had to travel a lot, you know. I've been alone in hotel rooms, so far from home, sad beyond words. Sure, I've had my flings, but without a family, what's it all worth? Family's what's important, damn it, so keep the family together!"

A few days later, I am on the highway that leads from San Salvador to the airport. Once again, I make the trip alone. It was a typical goodbye—wordless hugs on all sides. The highway stretches out before me; the Pacific appears as a gauzy blue ribbon on the horizon.

Grandfather, would you disown me if I joined up with the guerrillas? Uncle, why the fuck do you think there are young assailants after your gold? Pedro, I really should be with my family right now, this'll be the last beer, okay? By the way Pedro, or Roger or grandfather, are you certain that history is moving in a straight line here? A socialist utopia, a free-market paradise, intervention, attrition, quake after quake? Soledad, you are my age and our generation faces these impossible choices, and how can I advise you when I can neither face nor turn away from my own family? Grandfather, I watch your chest struggling to rise against the weight of these years. Why are you so quiet, grandfather? Maybe when the war is over, we can talk again. But you won't live that long . . .

The taxi rattles along the highway. The hot, humid sea air pours through the open windows as we pass by a column of soldiers marching along in sloppy formation before an expanse of charred cornfields. As we near the airport, I look back one last time through the rear window at the road that leads back to the hills, back to San Salvador, to the families that I am at once a part of and so distant from. Above those hills, towering, gleaming white clouds have gathered. But it's not going to rain, I tell myself. The rains are still months away . . .

L.A. Journal (II)

May 1990

"The authorities would have us do or would force us to do something against God's will," the priest says from the pulpit. "And when we don't do as they wish, they punish us or murder us, all because of our fidelity to His Law."

The church is filled to capacity, and the overflow crowd spills out onto the courtyard, where a loudspeaker crackles with the priest's voice. The air is hot, humid, heavy with the scent of human sweat. The parishioners fan themselves fervently with folded parish announcement sheets. "In our times, we have the example of Salvadoran archbishop Oscar Arnulfo Romero," the priest continues, his voice booming through the church. "Romero said things that didn't sit well with the government and with the military. . . . Three days before he was assassinated, he asked President Carter to stop sending more money to the military. Three days later, while he officiated the holy Mass, he was brutally assassinated before the altar of the Eucharist, and the blood of Romero mixed with the blood of Christ.

"This community of La Placita has distinguished itself by its preferential option for the poor. And the *migra* doesn't like it, and the FBI doesn't like it, and many civic authorities don't like it, and many times our very own ecclesiastical authorities don't like what this community proclaims: the defense of the poor, of the rejected, of the undocumented. But it is because of this—precisely because of this—that this Christian community deserves respect. They can kill us, they can reject us . . . but this community will continue faithful in its commitment to the poor."

OLIVARES
La Placita 1990

La Placita today is not the church it was before the arrival of Father Luis Olivares in 1981. Back then, it still leaned towards a touristy quaintness and was mainly attended by the Chicano and Mexicano middle class. Today, the vast majority of the parishioners are recent arrivals—Mexicanos and Centroamericanos, many of whom already knew of the church and its controversial pastor long before they began their perilous journeys north. La Placita has become a mythic haven on the well-trodden, obstacle-strewn path to the American Dream. Olivares allows hundreds of refugees to sleep in the church at night. Coordinating with various activist groups and social agencies, La Placita offers free medical and dental services as well as English classes and legal advice on immigration. From the pulpit Olivares denounces human rights violations in Central America, and he regularly calls for an end to US intervention in the region.

Influenced by liberation theology icons like Romero and Brazilian bishop Pedro Casaldáliga, Olivares has gained the respect of his mostly working-class Mexican and Salvadoran parishioners, and the enmity of virtually every government agency in the city, not to mention vigilante reactionaries: he has even received threats from an L.A. branch of El Salvador's infamous death squads, who sent him a cryptic note calling him a "communist son of a bitch."

I feel not a little sense of historical justice that the rights of Latinos are today fervently defended by Olivares from the pulpit of L.A.'s oldest and largest Catholic parish. For L.A. history begins at La Placita—as does my own history. I cross the city dozens of times in a single week, but I must always return there, I must always go home—just as the successive waves of Mexicano immigrants have inevitably been drawn to La Placita since the battle began in the eighteenth century to see who would win control of the Los Angeles basin.

The church was founded on September 4, 1781 when a ragtag band of forty-four Native American, *mestizo* and African subjects of Spain, along with one man who claimed pure Spanish blood, stuck a flag in the dusty chaparral. The L.A. pop history image is of Spanish troubadors on Palomino horses sweeping castanet-snapping señoritas off their feet, but the *Californios* (as the Mexican ranchers of the nineteenth century were known) were actually *mestizo*, wannabe Iberians who cracked a whip over the region's majority population of poor Mexicanos and smattering of Native Americans. After the American occupation in 1848, La Placita's Mexican priests were replaced with European clerics who attempted to suppress the traditional *fiestas* and other "pagan" Mexican Catholic rituals. But the Mexican poor would not give up La Placita. Exasperated at being unable to stamp out the parish's stubborn *cultura popular*, middle-class Europeans built a cathedral for themselves several blocks to the south; La Placita remained the church of the poor. And the church has continued to be the site of battles between the old and the new L.A.: throughout the twentieth century, whenever the political times made it expedient to lay blame for the country's economic problems on "foreigners," immigration authorities rounded up thousands of undocumented Mexicans in surprise raids at La Placita.

The false Spanish mythos was part of denying L.A.'s Mexican past, a veil behind which Mexicans were alternately exploited and given the boot. Although it has waned in recent decades in favor of an equally Hollywoodized version of the Mexican past (mariachis are invited to play at virtually every official city welcoming ceremony), remnants of the Spanish mythos remained embedded in the city's psyche during my school years, enough so that every time the Los Angeles Unified School District conducted an "ethnic survey" and I was presented with the choice of "Anglo," "Mexican," "Asian," "Black" or "Other," I would check this last box and pencil in "Spanish." At a young age, I learned to try to be anything other than a "dirty Mexican." My Salvadoran consciousness, during that time, was hardly an issue: Central America did not exist as far as L.A. was concerned until the Sandinista Army rolled into Managua, the FMLN appeared close to achieving a similar triumph in San Salvador, and hundreds of thousands of Central Americans showed up on the streets of the *barrio* surrounding MacArthur Park, later christened *Pequeño Centroamérica* ("Little Central America").

Back then, as I watched the images of the Sandinistas on NBC, Y was still in high school. They had just given her her first weapon—9mm shit, but there was a mystique about arms in the guerrilla organizations and it meant a lot to her. She carried it in her purse at all times, often nonchalantly walking by soldiers armed with M-16s. She dreamed of and waited for *la ofensiva final*. But intra-factional revolutionary intrigue would lead her to disillusionment before long. The war sucked her in, spat her out—and she landed in L.A.

Talkin' 'Bout my Generation

Havana 1988

As our plane glides in for a smooth landing at José Martí International airport on our way to the Tenth Annual New Latin American Cinema Festival, we applaud. Two nights ago, our group of filmmakers, students and journalists boarded another rickety Soviet airliner in Mexico City and roared down the runway for an unusually long time. Just as the nose was finally lifting off the ground, BANG!—the jet slammed back down onto the runway. The pilot hit the brakes and the plane fishtailed as sparks and flames shot out from beneath the wings. The young Communist Youth cadres sitting behind me, who'd been on an exchange visit in Mexico, crossed themselves instinctively as the voice of death itself roared all around us. We came to a stop twenty-five feet from the end of the runway—twenty-five feet from being smashed into a million bits and crushing the residents of a poor *barrio* underneath fiery wreckage. We breathed a collective sigh of relief; the saints of the Revolution had intervened. As we exited the craft, the pilot appeared at the door to his cabin with a face drained of color. He fumbled for a cigarette and lit it with trembling hands: "I had two seconds to make a decision, *compañeros*. Lucky for all of us, I made the right one."

We arrive in Havana at the height of the festivities. As our *guagua* (the nickname for buses in Cuba) rambles along the well-paved road toward downtown, we break out a bottle and pass it around. Time to marvel: I'm here.

My main experience of the island over the years (besides the scant, slanted coverage offered by the US media) has been listening to fading, bootlegged tapes of Silvio Rodríguez and Pablo Milanes, two New Song *trovadores* who sing as much of love these days as they do of *la madre Revolución*. Then there's my recollection of the enthusiasm in the eyes of my Latin American Marxist friends whenever they spoke of Cuba's achievements in art, in medicine . . . the only country on the continent without homeless people! I have also read about the repression of gays in Cuba, and about the experience of Cuban poet Heberto Padilla, jailed for sedition shortly after winning the Casa de las Americas literary prize in the late sixties, a time when fierce ideological debate about artistic freedom broke out in the Communist Party. Nevertheless, the idealistic New Song lyrics about the heroes of the movement—Che Guevara, Haydée Santamaría, and, of course, Fidel—kept creeping into my mind's ear as our flight neared the island.

Romantic, then, my vision of Cuba: an island in the imagination that existed apart from the resentment of the Cuban *gusanos* in Miami and the machinations of the hotheads in the US State Department, apart from the realities of blockade, underdevelopment, socialist contradictions and dependence on the Soviet Union. And Havana *is* romantic, both in its Caribbean sensuality and in its socialist spirit, but my first impressions of the streets begin to flesh out a complexity no Cuban song I've ever heard has captured. We pass by rows of pre-revolutionary buildings, tall colonial-style windows and dramatic door frames in varying stages of decay after years of exposure to the sea air. The architecture changes mid-block, clashingly, to revolutionary-minimalist apartment housing. And changes again as we enter the Vedado district, where the echoes of the Mob era rise up thirty stories and more in the form of the old seaside hotels, such as the Havana Libre (once the Hilton) or the Capri, where legend has it that mobsters sliced up a cake shaped in the form of the island, thus symbolically devouring their backyard whorehouse (a scene Francis Ford Coppola included in *The Godfather, Part II*).

It is Saturday night in Havana. As we weave in and out of traffic that juxtaposes an inordinate number of finned Chevies and Buicks from the fifties with Soviet-made Ladas and World War Two vintage three-wheeled motorcycles with sidecars, huge crowds are gathering in front of the cinemas and at the local hangouts. Caribbean music blares out from a dozen different points on this Saturday night near the end of the twenty-ninth year of a revolution that began three years before I was born.

Mid-afternoon and things are quiet in the watch repair shop. The clerk is a middle-aged woman, just slightly over the edge, slowly being driven mad by the city's particular brand of neurosis: the overcrowded living conditions, the unbridled bureaucracy . . .

In walks a customer, a lean and grizzled old man. It seems the watch he bought here just days ago has already broken down. Can he have his money back? Now an attractive woman half the clerk's age steps into the store and silently watches the proceedings. The older woman says no, he can't have his money back. What about an exchange? (This'll make everything easier—less paperwork to be filed with the corresponding authorities.)

It is the young woman who protests: "You have to give him his money back! It's his right!" This is true, but the older woman doesn't like being contradicted by this upstart. The old man is now insisting on his refund. The clerk grudgingly fills out a new receipt as the young woman stalks out of the store. "Imagine," fumes the clerk. "The Revolution has given her everything, and she still has the nerve . . ."

"You're right," says the slightly senile compañero. "What a bunch of ungrateful kids we have today!"

The audience, the vast majority in their teens and twenties, roars with laughter at this exchange. Cuban director Juan Carlos Tabia, well known as a social critic after his highly successful satire *Se Permuta* (which dealt with the effects of Havana's severe housing crisis), is at it again in his latest film, *Plaff!* (an onomatopoeic term denoting the central metaphor of the film: eggs hurled—plaff!—at outdated Cuban attitudes and institutions).

Laughing especially hard is the young man sitting next to me. Camilo, a 28-year-old video artist who works at the Cuban Institute for Radio and Television (ICRT), sees in *Plaff!* the kind of commentary that he wishes were more a part of Cuban media today. Cuban TV has tended to lag behind the cinematic vanguard, he tells me. And there are only two stations to cover the needs of the island's estimated ten million viewers.

"Let's be honest," Camilo tells me in the lobby after the screening. "The situation's terrible."

My main experience of Cuban television since arriving here has been of overdubbed Soviet cartoons, reruns of 1960s kiddie TV fare like *Flipper,* and newscasts and talk shows dominated by reports on the country's agricultural and industrial production. Then there are a couple of imported *telenovelas* (soap operas) and some awkward attempts to reach Cuban youth via shows like *Joven Joven*, a cross between US rock 'n' roll shows like *American Bandstand* and MTV. And, of course, there's *Palabras de Fidel,* minute-long snippets from the Commandante's Greatest Hits speeches. The only bright spot is the occasional classic Latin American film.

What is needed is a new approach, Camilo tells me. He has a term to describe *his* aesthetic—*ganas de joder* (the "desire to fuck around," create a stir). "TV after the Revolution," he says, "assumed a narrow moralism and an antagonism toward its audience." Add to this the ever-present specter of bureaucratic inertia and cultural paternalism, and you've got retro TV.

Take, for example, the commercials intended to promote internal tourism by drawing Cubans to their own beaches. These clips are riddled with First World clichés: beautiful blondes basking in the sun, windsurfers, et cetera. "It promotes the same consumerist culture we are supposedly trying to finish off!" Camilo will play off this irony in his next project—a video satirizing the commercials.

"I want to produce a more faithful representation of Cuban reality," Camilo says, snuffing out a filterless *Popular* cigarette as he gets up to enter the theater for the next festival feature. "That's the spirit of these times. It's not a complete break with the past, but a critical-birth." And already, he says, it's starting to happen. Young video artists have started experimenting with music videos, fictional shorts and the like. But time is running out. Camilo wants to see exchange with young artists the world over, new technology, more experimentation—now. "Because in twelve years," he says, "we'll all be from the past century."

I meet Graciela at a festival-sponsored seminar titled "The Eighties Generation" held at the Palacio de las convenciones, a huge complex on the outskirts of town. We sit in a temperature-controlled, Olympic-size auditorium, sterile as a forensics lab. The speakers sit on a raised platform above us and read from prepared texts.

Graciela listens intently as each lecturer details the woes of "the Latin American crisis" (social, economic, aesthetic), and as each affirms his or her commitment to making things better. I recall the seminar scene from Cuban director Tomás Gutiérrez Alea's 1972 *Memorias del subdesarrollo* (Memories of Underdevelopment) in which the stuffy elitism of the lecturers has heads nodding until an American in the crowd, the playwright Jack Gelber, asks: "Why is it the Cuban Revolution . . . has to resort to an archaic form of discussion such as a roundtable and treat us to an impotent discussion of issues that I'm well informed about, and most of the public here is well informed about, when there could be another more revolutionary way to reach an audience like this?" The critique was made a quarter of a century ago. Yet here we are today, still listening to the blah-blah-blah. Some things about the New Latin American Cinema aren't so new.

Later, Graciela sits across the table from me at Coppelia, a park in the center of the Vedado district. It is mid-afternoon, and young couples lounge on the tables in front of the ice cream and food stands. Just as we are about to sit down, a young black man, dressed rather shabbily by Cuban standards, beckons me. He's offering pesos for dollars. *Buen precio.* "Don't pay attention to him," Graciela warns me, and we sit down.

Born in 1964, Graciela, a mulatta with short hair and brown eyes that give off a hint of green when she looks toward the light, is quite conscious of her "*pos-Girón*" (post Bay of Pigs) generational standing, using the collective "we" when she speaks about people her age.

Cuba is changing, she tells me. "We didn't live the events of 1959. *Los viejos* think that what's important is for us to learn about the events that led up to 1959. But what's important is what's happening today. When you're young, you want to see your ideas, your worries and dreams reflected in society, in the media."

Of course, this does not happen. Although there are several daily newspapers, each of them targeting a different segment of Cuban society—urban workers, *campesinos*, women, youth, et cetera—none is probing deep enough, Graciela tells me, into the issues that matter to most Cubans today. And there's no lack of problems to deal with. Crime? "You hear about it all the time." Prostitution? "Just go to any of the hotels in the Vedado." Public transportation? "I have to spend two hours getting to and from work sometimes." Overcrowding, lack of access to consumer goods, long queues . . . If the Cuban press doesn't begin to deal more openly with these issues, Graciela says, people will be looking to other sources. "Already there's Radio Martí," she notes. "And now there's talk of TV Martí."

Graciela assures me that capitalism is not the cure. The answer, she says, lies in Fidel's campaign of *rectificación,* begun in early 1986—the rectification of errors that the Revolution itself has committed over the years. And it's *rectificación,* not *glasnost.* Fidel seems reluctant even to utter the Russian word. Yet the very candor with which Graciela is talking to me about these issues constitutes something akin to the new Soviet "openness" and reflects the change in the Cuban spirit she has been describing. I will encounter this kind of frankness again and again during my stay. A few days earlier, a Cuban art critic I spoke with had put it this way: "What we have in Cuba today is a *glasnost* that can't say its name."

I've been here four days now and have yet to leave the Vedado district. Unexpectedly, a friend from the festival asks if I'd like to visit her relatives, who live on the outskirts of town. I jump at the chance.

Crossing the city from the Vedado district to Barrio Belen is akin to crossing over the border into Mexico at Tijuana: older housing, potholes to avoid, plenty of dust. There are fewer late-model Soviet cars here, more fintailed antiques. The García family has lived here in the same tall-ceilinged colonial-style house since before the Revolution. Today, four generations share the space here: a matriarchal great-grandmother, her son and his wife, their two sons and their wives and children—a dozen people in all. Chairs and couches crowd even the hallways, along with sepia photographs, model Aeroflot jetliners and pre-revolutionary dolls, dusty and mute. A veritable museum.

And although this is a *barrio,* the Garcías don't live badly at all—TV, VCR, stereo equipment, numerous electric appliances. Both sons have worked in the merchant marine. Jobs that land your sons on foreign shores—and thus put them within reach of goods not readily available in Cuba—tend to make life somewhat easier. But make no mistake, the Garcías don't consider themselves capitalists. In this household, no one needs to be prodded into defending the Revolution and its gains. Tony,

CRUISING HAVANA

the younger of the two sons, is a longtime cadre of the Communist Youth organization. His brother is a veteran of Cuba's Angola campaign.

Rectificación will take care of the imperfections, Tony tells me. "We're not perfect, so there'll always be imperfections." And ever newer phases of rectification. But he does see a problem these days with some of the younger kids. Some—he emphasizes that they aren't many, just some— are straying off the path. Listening to rock-'n'-roll. Wearing earrings. "What do I know about it? Look for sex, doing drugs . . ." Rock, and all the values that it espouses, says Tony, are "poisoning" the young.

"They're the ones that are out playing hooky, the ones with the empty minds. And the worst thing is, they're not contributing anything to the Revolution. The Revolution has given them everything, but what are they giving in return?"

We are treated to a lunch of steak, salad and fruit. I'm tempted to ask how they managed such a feast in a country where most people eat red meat only a few times a year, but I don't. Later Tony gives us a ride back into town. We hop into his 1954 Buick (original motor, but jerry-rigged with a Japanese starter and Soviet alternator). Before he starts the car, Tony pulls a pair of Ray Ban shades out of his shirt pocket and slips them on. The ancient motor growls awake, and we float out onto the streets of the *barrio*.

Today a frigid wind rushes up the seaside avenues, whipping the festival flags. The sky is overcast and dark clouds threaten rain. Despite being so close to the equator, Cuba appears to have caught the tail end of the northern hemisphere's winter.

But this spot of bad weather doesn't dampen the Cubans' enthusiasm for their festival. I stand in a line about five hundred strong outside the Yara theater, waiting for the screening of the Argentine film *Sur* by Fernando Solanas, which everyone predicts will sweep the awards. (It does.) Because there are so many patrons, a squad of Revolutionary Police have been summoned for crowd control. The fans press forward, impatient. The police scowl and blow their whistles.

Ahead of me in line, sneezing loudly, is a Cuban teenager, burrowed deep inside a heavy jacket, obviously in the grip of a bad attack of flu. Pablo is every inch an adolescent, his light complexion reddened by acne, his unruly hair verging on being what's considered "long" here. The more I find out about him, the more I realize I'm talking to a genuine child of the Revolution. He's seventeen, still in high school, and sure of one thing at least: he's no good at math. But he's interested in literature, the arts and, of course, cinema. Just this morning he was at the hospital with his mother, waiting for a prescription for his flu. She had begged him to stay home and rest. But he couldn't possibly miss *Sur*!

As soon as he finds out that I live in the States, the interrogation begins. Have I heard the music of Metallica? His enthusiasm boils over when he finds out that the newspaper I work for recently published an interview with that heavy-metal music group. The way Pablo tells it, someone somewhere along the line got an album from someone in the States. The bootlegging since then has been legendary. And that's not all. He recently bought a poster of Kiss—do I know their music?—for twenty Cuban pesos (about $18) on the black market.

But it's not easy being a rock fan in Cuba. "Tight pants and long hair aren't too popular with *los viejos*." Our conversation is interrupted again by the piercing screech of the Revolutionary Police whistles. "Please move back. Move back! We won't let anyone else in until you start behaving like adults!" The crowd relents and eases the forward pressure for a moment. But not for long.

Pablo tells me he had the honor of being detained recently by the police. At a rock concert, no less. Seems that the party got a little too loose. The paddy wagons hauled off several kids and treated them to a mild, if uncomfortable and absurd, interrogation.

"They asked me such stupid questions," recalls Pablo, "about why I wear tight pants, if I like easy women, if I do drugs. They think rock means all that. Why do I like rock? I just do. I don't have to explain myself to them. Liking rock doesn't mean you're a *desviado* [deviate]." Why, there are perfectly decent people walking around, well-dressed people, people who can cite Lenin verbatim and who really are deviates.

The crowd pushes forward another few feet, and suddenly we've slipped past the ropes and into the theater. As we go through the glass doors, the police whistles go off again. The theater is already nearly full as we walk in and find our seats. Pablo quickly scans the faces of the people seated around us. Then he leans close and says, "There's something I want to ask you about. Everybody talks about it, but not in public. Is it true that TV Marti will be going on the air soon?" He's obviously disappointed when I tell him I don't know.

An adventure against the established order—in this lies the wisdom of this school. That is, if it has one. The creative adventure against the order we've inherited. The death of the stereotypes of the New Latin American Cinema; the search of the current and future generations—like the fruit of our old political and poetic struggles for the liberation of our identity—has the right to be, the obligation to be, vital and continental and without adjectives: The Latin American Cinema . . .

Fernando Birri, Director, EICTV

The campus of the International Film and Television School (EICTV) lies in the midst of jungle about an hour from downtown Havana. One hundred and twenty students from three worlds (as opposed to the Third World)—Latin America, Asia and Africa—have access here not only to state-of-the-art equipment, but to top filmmakers who come here to teach from all over the globe.

In his sixties, with a pepper-gray beard that drapes halfway down his chest, and long hair pulled back into a ponytail, Fernando Birri, a co-founder of the New Latin American Cinema movement, relishes controversy. Indeed, his new film, an adaptation of Gabriel García Márquez's short story "A Very Old Man With Enormous Wings," has come close to causing a critical riot here. The disjunctive narrative structure and his inclusion in the film of a rock video have resulted in more than a few nasty epithets ("You've sold out to the *gringos,* Birri!").

Undaunted, the maverick director says the furor has him feeling like he's "started his career all over again." Then there's the volatility of the school that he directs. Students have produced films dealing with sensitive Cuban issues, such as the personality cult of Fidel, homophobia, and the kids who listen to rock 'n' roll. Birri defends the independence of the school, and enjoys citing Fidel on culture to fend off his critics: "The enemy is not abstract art, but imperialism." He is held in almost universally high regard by the students at the school.

EICTV has gained quite a reputation among locals unused to hordes of art kids out on filmic excursions, probing the Cuban culture with camera and questions asked in all manner of foreign accents. Legend has it that one local called the school "a ship of fools," and Birri, upon hearing the comment, immediately decided to make it the school's motto.

For Wolney Mattos, a 28-year-old student from Brazil, EICTV is all about pluralism. Witness the diversity: the students at the school early on split into subgroups: "postmodernists," "leftists" and "rightists" (as the formalist-centrists are called by the hard-line leftists). Birri has called the school "a revolution within the [Cuban] Revolution." Mattos agrees. "The most important thing for our generation, I believe, is *perestroika*, a re-evaluation of not only the sixties, but also the fifties, the forties—all the generations that preceded us."

INT. NIGHT

We are in the comfortable apartment of the Montalba family in the Miramar district. There is art on the walls, and hundreds of books on the shelves. The family—father José, a technician at the Cuban Institute of Cinematographic Art and Industry (ICAIC); mother Elsa, a schoolteacher; and her brother Daniel, a computer technician—sit at the dining room table along with me and Alejandro, a Uruguayan EICTV student whom they've befriended. The two teenage children of José and Elsa have locked themselves in their rooms to listen to records: heavy metal and Julio Iglesias, respectively.

Alejandro has brought three documentaries home from school to screen for me. This is not the first time the Montalbas have hosted such screenings. A bottle of rum is opened, cigarettes are lit, but before the lights go down . . .

ELSA
(taking a drag)

I'm not worried about the kids listening to rock. It's just a phase;

they'll grow out of it. What happens here is that things are talked about always in ideological terms: "This is *yanqui*," "That's the enemy," "That's ideological penetration." If we were friends with the US, none of this would be happening.

DANIEL
(assuming a professorial air)

It's true that rock has an aggressive attitude behind it. But remember the socioeconomic context. Rock isn't the cause of aggression; it only helps to let off steam where there is already aggression.

ELSA

Young people today have different needs than we did. For us, a pair of shoes was a lot. For these kids, it's a personal computer.

DANIEL
(sternly)

But don't think that everyone here thinks like us. Be careful about making generalizations when you write your article.

ALEJANDRO
(enthusiastic)

A majority of the intelligentsia think this way, though.

ELSA

The documentaries the students have made . . . I'll tell you, when I see them, I think, "How great! But what a shame no Cuban is doing such work."

JOSÉ
(quietly)

But things are changing. You can criticize the Revolution from within today; you can be revolutionary and not be in agreement with the Party. The very conversation we're having with you tonight would not have been possible two years ago.

RUBÉN

So this is a version of *glasnost*? *Perestroika*?

DANIEL

No . . . I mean, yes. It is *perestroika*, but it's not *perestroika*. Know what I mean?

ELSA

Listen. We're being very honest with you, very open, without knowing who you are, who you work for. We've told you everything we can tell you. There are some things we can't tell you, though. You'd have to live here a long time to understand.

RUBÉN

So I can use your real names for the article?

Silence for a few beats. Everyone around the table exchanges glances.

ELSA

If we knew you better . . . Well, maybe you'd better not.

DANIEL
(changing the subject)
You live in Los Angeles, right? The Dodgers, right? That home run by Gibson was incredible, wasn't it? But I still like the Oakland As. José Canseco—did you know that he's Cuban?

FADE OUT

FADE IN

Dozens of screens glowing with images all at once, different incarnations of one man—Fidel Castro. Fidel raging in a speech, Fidel young, Fidel older. Historic moments of the past thirty years: Fidel in the Sierra Maestra, plotting the revolution with Che Guevara; Fidel saying that no one but no

one has the right to come in and inspect Cuba for missiles; Fidel the hardliner,
"Within the Revolution, everything; outside the Revolution, nothing."

   There follow several classic person-on-the-street interviews. One question
only: "What do you think will happen in Cuba when Fidel's no longer
around?"

   "That would be unreal!"

   "It would be an irreparable loss."

   "What do you mean? Fidel will always be here, even when he's dead!"

from *All Men Are Mortal*, a documentary directed by
Argentine film student Christa María Civale

Those of us who have neckties strangle ourselves into them. Others stick to
their jeans and safari jackets. A caravan of *guaguas* brings thousands of
festivalgoers to the mammoth monolith that is the Palacio de la Revolución. We enter the palace, dwarfed beneath a ceiling as tall as any colonial
cathedral. We gorge ourselves on a sumptuous spread of assorted meats and
cheeses, fine Soviet wine (really, it's good!) and, of course, Cuban rum.
Slowly, word gets around that the Commandate is ensconced in a VIP
reception area off to the side of the main room. People gather around the
wood-slatted partition, straining to catch a glimpse of beard. When the
doors finally open the crowd surges forward, exclaiming, "It's him! It's
him!" He shakes hands. Strokes cheeks. Pats shoulders and backs. Smiles
and makes small talk.

   Thirty-five years ago, when Fidel and the original Twenty-sixth of July
Movement staged their first failed uprising, he was twenty-six years old (my
age); he is sixty-two today, slightly pale, a little on the pudgy side (maybe
he gained weight after he gave up cigars?). The circles under his eyes have
grown wrinkles.

   The idea of entering the third decade of the Cuban Revolution is
probably adding to those wrinkles. In the *rectificación* speeches of the last
two years, he has consistently criticized what he deems backsliding.
Economic experiments such as the Peasant Free Market led to the creation of
a small, prosperous class that hoarded product and demanded outrageous
prices. Fewer and fewer people turned up for voluntary work brigades.
Production levels fell off. People wanted to "work less for more money," the
Commandante lamented.

Cuba today is facing more than its share of contradictions, and Fidel continues to foment a nationalistic, defensive posture among the cadres of the Revolution, an implicit reminder that "the Empire" is still only ninety miles from home.

"The enemy never ceases to work [on] the ideological front, in its campaigns against our nation abroad as well as within the country. Not in vain does it invest all possible resources to soften up our people and present as an idyllic image its consumerist society." So spake Fidel on December 5, the words booming out across the Plaza de la Revolución before the cadres. "Under these circumstances it's more important than ever before to strengthen confidence in the Party. . . . It is the duty of our Revolution to give the party more and more authority . . . Today, more than ever, discipline is indispensable. All who promote or participate in social indiscipline are championing the enemy. They are conscious or unconscious agents of the enemy."

As I read the text of Fidel's speech, I find myself looking for a word on culture or the youth, something that will fulfill, as Graciela put it, the need to see her worries, desires, dreams commented upon openly by the Party. But, despite the fact that Fidel has pledged that *rectificación* will not lead to *extremismo*—no cultural revolution à la Chairman Mao—there is still no clear evidence of an opening that would allow youth and the intelligentsia to freely explore international culture without having a run-in with overzealous Party bureaucrats.

After the reception, the crowd files back into the *guaguas*, and we are shuttled to Cristino's, a huge complex like a country club that was once the playground of the Cuban bourgeoisie. I wander from ballroom to ballroom under the huge crystal chandeliers. First, a young, long-haired New Song singer croons plaintively à la Silvio Rodríguez. Then, disco music pulses through the speakers. Upstairs, everyone's sitting cross-legged on the floor, listening to Cuba's premier Latin jazz trumpeter, Arturo Sandoval. Outside, on a dance floor the size of a football field (and still there's not enough room for everyone), the hottest salsa I have ever heard has worked tourists and Cuban teenagers alike into a sensual frenzy. Young Cubans have developed an erotic dance style highly suggestive of specific sexual acts—the girls and guys virtually simulate oral copulation—yet another "problem" cited by the moral authorities of the Party.

The festival is over. Tomorrow, it's back to the First World. I walk around, not knowing anyone, not talking to anyone, just watching. All the scenes taken together—the disco, the salsa, the jazz, the New Song—create a mosaic as wild as anything I've seen in Mexico City, the most cosmopolitan city in Latin America.

I walk to the edge of the outdoor dancing area. Behind me, thousands of bodies are caught up in the celebration. Before me, the Caribbean Sea shimmers in the moonlight. Only ninety miles away, I tell myself. A strong, cold wind is blowing, and I have a crazy impulse to jump into the balmy water. Instead, I turn around, realizing that more than anything else, I want to dive back into Cristino's and dance to all those rhythms at once.

L.A. Journal (III)

June 1990

Today, a piercing blue sky: the famous Santa Ana Winds have returned
with their dry cowboy heat and blown the smog out to sea. Y and I awake
slightly hungover, in my father's old bedroom in my late grandparents'
house in Silver Lake, amid the moving boxes and dust from the
destruction/construction that's taking place inside and outside. Carpen-
ters have taken sledgehammers and sandblasters to the walls: the past is
crumbling. Father and I had bickered over the remodelling plans. Father
the modernizer, I the preservationist. Father won.

Last night, Y and I weaved home drunk and made love in the same
room where my father once watched searchlights crisscross the sky during
the air-raid blackouts of World War Two, and perhaps pinned up
magazine shots of a leggy Betty Grable. (Father told me recently that my
sleeping here with a woman who is not yet my wife is probably enough to
make grandmother turn over in her grave.) We had partied with what's
left of the Salvadoran revolutionary cadres-in-exile. Famous guerrilla-salsa
band Chiltic-Istac played (they're nine-year veterans of the L.A. exile
scene) and without a trace of irony led the crowd in slogan-spiked *cumbias*
("*Si Nicaragua venció, El Salvador vencerá! Y Guatemala!*"). I made a point
of not mentioning the Nicaraguan election; nobody mentioned it. What
was unspoken was the obvious. There will be no *victoria final*, no
triumphant FMLN entry into San Salvador and the subsequent return of
the exiles to work in mass literacy programs or to wield machetes
alongside the *campesinos*. Our generation—Y and I were highschool age

67

when we watched the Sandinistas roll into Managua on TV—has paid in blood for a revolution that not only will not be televised, but probably won't even be remembered as a revolution at all.

We straggle out of bed and arrive at La Placita just in time for the 11:30 Mass. Y and I make our way through a sidewalk crowded with dozens of street vendors selling bootlegged cassettes, *tamales*, *champurrado*, blinking plastic roses. I'd been fantasizing for some time that Y and I would finally finish our five years of coming together and falling apart (her leaving for Guatemala, my following her, my returning to L.A., her following me) by getting married here at La Placita, with pastor Father Luis Olivares offering the vows.

But Olivares will most likely not offer us our vows. The superiors of the Claretian Order have announced that Olivares will be transfered to a Fort Worth parish, a move widely interpreted as politically motivated. Only two weeks before his scheduled departure, he fell ill with what was initially diagnosed as meningitis with complications. This Sunday was to have been Olivares's farewell, but we have been told that he is still hospitalized, in a serious condition.

We enter the church and squirm in through the typical over-capacity crowd. To our surprise, we see Olivares at his usual post, seated beneath the large image of the Virgen de Guadalupe to the left of the altar. His head is bowed with exhaustion, and he still wears a hospital identity bracelet. He cradles his head in pain. Associate pastor Michael Kennedy officiates the Mass, but for the homily he hands the microphone to Olivares, who can barely hold it with his pale, trembling hands. His voice begins in a whisper, but soon he is weaving a powerful and emotional sermon. He confides that the doctors have given him one or two years to live. "But I do not fear death, my brothers and sisters. One must accept the will of God. If He wants me stay on in this, this," he summons a weak, somewhat ironic smile before going on, "vale of tears, then I will stay. If He wishes me to leave, I will leave."

Father Luis Olivares bids La Placita farewell with these words: "Like John the Baptist was called . . . so each of us, upon being baptized, is called to be a prophet of love and justice. I ask the Lord for a special blessing for this community that has fought so hard for justice, not only here and in Central America, but all over the world. May it continue to do so, to live out the true meaning of the Gospel." He sinks back into the wheelchair, exhausted.

After the recitation of the Lord's Prayer, during the offering of peace, an old Mexicana painfully canes her way up to the altar to touch Olivares. Next, a communion-aged boy does the same. Soon, a crowd of parishioners is tearfully laying hands upon him. Then a tall, attractive blonde woman who has been standing near Olivares (who also has a bastion of support among the Hollywood Hip Crowd) puts a stop to this. Towering over the children and *ancianos* she tells them, "*No más, no más,*" in a thickly accented Spanish. In the midst of this agonizing scene, Y and I take communion from the hands of Father Michael Kennedy. We return to the pews and kneel to pray as we watch Olivares being wheeled away. I summon the childhood *oraciones*, but find myself stumbling over the words.

Five days later, during my morning ritual at my late grandmother's house, I open the front door and pick up the morning edition of the *Los Angeles Times*. I scan the local news:

ACTIVIST PRIEST SAYS HE HAS AIDS

Father Luis Olivares, the activist Roman Catholic priest and long-time champion of Central American refugees who had been hospitalized for the past month with meningitis, revealed Thursday that he has AIDS. Doctors said they believe that he contracted the disease from contaminated needles while undergoing treatment for other ailments while traveling in Central America. . . .

A Death in the Family

Los Angeles, March 1988

Sergio is wearing jeans with two jagged holes at the knees, a T-shirt with suspenders, and a red bandana headband: he's both punk and vato. His face is expressive and mercurial: a hard look gives way to a quirky smile, blends into a distant gaze.

Daniel Lara presses the fast-forward button on the VCR. He eases himself back in his chair and props his head upon his hand, silently watching the accelerated images of Sergio's birthday party ripple across the screen. He says that he is looking for a specific image that will show me Sergio "at his best." He lets the tape roll at normal speed for a few moments.

Sergio's family and friends are gathered in the backyard of a modest barrio home on a sunny afternoon. The children shout and dash about. Someone puts on some music—a cumbia rhythm. Sergio beams. He gets up to dance.

"This is what I wanted you to see," says Daniel.

Only a few people follow Sergio's lead. The rest are still seated, content to watch. As he bends his knees, his skin shows through the holes in his Levis. He smiles, tosses his head back like an outrageously proud macho, and then he swings his hips exaggeratedly, sensually.

"Isn't that incredible?" says Daniel. "Here he is, being, what's the word? So *fruity*. And yet his family—they're completely okay with it!"

Closeups on the faces of the family members seated around the impromptu dance floor. There is some laughter, perhaps from mild embarrassment, but not a single face betrays ill feelings. Sergio closes his eyes, stretches his arms wide, opens his palms and twirls about . . .

The offices of AIDS Project Los Angeles (APLA) don't exactly make you feel you're in a protective environment; they have a corporate feel to them, and you could mistake the ambience for that of an insurance firm. In Daniel Lara's office (he is program manager for community education here) the strains of a Mexican *balada* emerge from a small tape deck. Atop a small end table, there is more of Mexico: potted cactus plants and some pre-Columbian figurines.

Daniel had met Sergio five years ago, and soon afterward they began living together, he tells me, his face slightly pale above the growth of a new beard. They had come from completely different worlds. Sergio grew up in Mexico City's *barrios*, a boy who became aware of being different at an early age. And it was as if Sergio's very body was at the center of the relentless conflict of growing up gay in such an eminently anti-gay environment as Mexico—from his early years, he suffered from numerous physical maladies. At age ten, there was rheumatic fever. Before he was out of his teens, he'd suffered a heart attack. Later there was open heart surgery, two strokes.

"He knew that if he were ever going to be truly happy with himself, he would have to be somewhere where he could be free of the prejudices and negative stereotypes about gay men in Mexico," says Daniel.

In coming to Los Angeles and meeting Daniel, Sergio had been able to establish his independence firmly. But that success had not been achieved overnight. Once here, Sergio followed a path familiar to many, if not most, Latin American immigrants. Although he finished a *preparatoria* education in Mexico (equivalent to junior college in the United States) and attained a degree in accounting, the language barrier and the fact that his credentials weren't transferable meant that Sergio found himself on the bottom rung of the socioeconomic ladder. He worked as a short-order cook at a Burrito King to make ends meet. But his ambitious nature led him to take night courses at Roosevelt Bilingual School, where he polished his English. Classes at East Los Angeles College came next. His goal was a management-level job.

When finally he landed a job as a telephone operator at the Department of Motor Vehicles (DMV), it wasn't exactly management, but it was a start. Sergio fell ill around that time, however. Although he soon recovered from what he would later discover had been the beginning of an

ARC (AIDS-Related Complex) condition, he lost his job at the DMV. The official diagnosis of full-blown AIDS came in August 1986.

"He looked at AIDS—and I've never been able to reconcile myself with this—as a gift," says Daniel. "He said that AIDS for him was an affirmation, a sign that God had not abandoned him." Sergio's traditional Catholicism—highly ironic, considering the Church's official anti-gay attitude—was a catalyst for Daniel. He had grown up in the States and flirted with Chicano Movement politics in its heyday, but had ultimately opted for a secular and professional existence well within the American mainstream. Meeting Sergio, Daniel says, was like "hitting a brick wall."

"He was very tied to religion. He had his *velas* [votive candles], and he had his *santos* [Saints], and he had his *medallas* [religious medallions], his *hierbas*, his holy water and his *oraciones*; all of these were things that I'd lost." Daniel smiles as he recites the list in Spanish. "I now have the *velas*, I have Sergio's *santos*, I have his *hierbas*."

When Sergio's mother came up from Mexico City to visit her son soon after his AIDS diagnosis, she faced his homosexuality openly for the first time. She told him that she would not speak to him until after he "changed his lifestyle," Daniel remembers. More than a year would pass without contact between mother and son. Sergio's father never knew about his son's gay lifestyle, nor would he ever learn that he had AIDS.

As his health worsened, Sergio came more and more into contact with a health establishment little prepared to handle the AIDS crisis. At the time of his diagnosis, APLA was practically the only resource available to persons with AIDS, regardless of ethnic or class background. And in Sergio's view, APLA was doing little, if anything at all, for Latinos with AIDS. He began to complain—to anyone who'd listen—about what he saw as a discriminatory situation.

Sergio's illness and activist sentiment spurred Daniel to take action by offering his services to APLA. Although the agency is considered by many activists to be part of the AIDS "establishment," Daniel felt that the best way to influence it was by working within the system, accepting its sometimes sluggish nature. But Sergio, always the rebel, took the opposite approach.

"Whereas we would say, 'You have to deal with the system,' he would

LATINO AIDS VIGIL
Los Angeles 1988

say, 'No you don't, you can fight.'" Sergio often went straight to APLA's top administration—over Daniel's head—demanding, among other things, that APLA bilingualize its services. Sergio also lobbied for bereavement counseling in Spanish to help an AIDS victim's family deal with the impact of the disease, something he considered essential for family-oriented Latino culture and its particular brand of homophobia.

Sergio literally took his message to the streets. He gave dozens of public *platicas*, informal talks, on AIDS at churches, schools, hospitals, "anywhere they'd take us," says Daniel. He would talk about his life experiences, about the poor treatment he'd received in hospitals, about the need for more education and AIDS services for Latinos. But most important, says Daniel, Sergio's message was "that his goal was to live, and, cliché as it sounds, that AIDS was the disease, and that faith was the cure."

In the fall, Daniel began noticing that Sergio was suffering lapses of memory and other signs of dementia. Still, Sergio mustered enough strength to join the hundreds of thousands of gay men and women who marched on Washington, DC in October, calling for a government response to the AIDS crisis.

It was in November, Daniel says, that he lost the Sergio he'd known and loved. By December, Sergio was bedridden, almost continually delirious. Daniel phoned Sergio's mother in Mexico City and she was soon at her son's bedside, no longer complaining about his "lifestyle" but taking care of his every need as she did when he was a baby.

Sergio's mother and Daniel decided to place him on a morphine drip, without any other treatment, as a way of letting him die without any more unnecessary suffering. On December 12, a traditional Mexican holiday in honor of the Virgen de Guadalupe, Sergio was lucid for a few hours. Daniel took the opportunity to tell him of their decision. "He put both of his hands on my face," Daniel says, now placing his hands on his cheeks. "He said to me, 'How can you help me to live, if you are so negative? You have to believe me when I tell you that I will get over this, that this will pass, and I can't do it unless you're on my side.'"

One day in early January, Sergio told Daniel: "You don't believe me when I tell you that I won't die." In retrospect, Daniel says, "I think he meant it in the spiritual sense. That his spirit would continue to be here. I only focused on the physical."

` Sergio died the next day.

At the service, there was anything but morbidity. Daniel had wanted a celebration, and there indeed was one, with mariachi music and a large gathering of friends. Daniel had thought that only such a ceremony would befit what Sergio would surely have believed was his passing into the Afterlife.

Daniel boarded the plane in Los Angeles dressed in black. Sergio's family greeted him at the airport in Mexico City dressed in black. He had known that the "celebration of life" in L.A. was the opposite of what he would encounter in Mexico. The open grief that he found among Sergio's family was anathema to Daniel. He feared that if he gave in to the sorrow, he wouldn't be able to control himself . . . and then what? Have the family about him wonder why he cried like a wife over a dead husband?

Daniel accompanied Sergio's family and friends to the mausoleum to place the ashes in the crypt. En route, he carried the box containing the ashes in his lap. He held it all the way to the mausoleum, causing an invisible but extremely uncomfortable tension between him and Sergio's mother.

"May I have my son?" she asked Daniel in front of the crypt.

Daniel hesitated. He ran his hand along the box, and slowly handed it to her. She placed the ashes in the crypt, knelt and said her goodbyes. Sergio's father did the same, then his sister. Two workers were about to set in place the stone that would seal the crypt forever when Daniel asked them to wait. He knelt down, and with his hand reached into the space for a moment, as if to retrieve Sergio. But his hand came out empty, and with it he drew the sign of the cross before the crypt.

La Distancia

For Tony: In Memoriam

Querida Y:

Last night was not a second;
that millennium with you is now my life.
I will remember you often . . .
As I write this, I sit
in yet another airport lobby,
waiting. The smog hangs
over the tarmac and the pall
bearers lift the city up.
I imagine the name
of the airline changes and that
I am on my way home.
Or to Paris.
Or to any impossible city like that.
Our tropical sea still lies
thousands of miles away (and such
a treacherous road!), while
a few hundred miles south,
they wait at the border,
readying to battle the dust
and come north.
I dream of walking south
to meet them, convince them

to return home and dream
away the war
(and then live the dream).
I envision the wind before
a deluge in El Salvador—
that terrifying liberation.
For now, I leave the north
to arrive in the north.
And you, of course, are leaving
the south to arrive . . .
Y, why are we always leaving
to arrive nowhere?

Te recuerda,
R

L.A. Journal (IV)

August 1990

Thunderheads towered over the mountains today, and humidity engulfed
the city. At nightfall, lightning flashed over Glendale, Silver Lake, Los
Feliz and Echo Park—a virtually unheard of occurrence during the L.A.
summer. The storm clouds that cut the full moon in half took me back to
San Salvador where, as a boy, I was enthralled by the thunder showers that
descended upon the city every evening in the winter. The clouds would
rush down the slopes of the volcano accompanied by wild winds and
lightning that often struck close enough for me to smell the seared air. I
knew that in Central America this afternoon the clouds would be building
up as always, even as they did so here. I called Y, for the first time since
she had returned to Guatemala. I punched the number fruitlessly a couple
of dozen times, only to get the recorded message, "We're sorry, all
circuits to the country you dialed are busy . . ." One hundred thousand or
so other Centroamericanos across the city were also trying the numbers of
their loved ones; today is Sunday. Sunday is family day, Sunday is
nostalgia. Sunday is I don't give a damn if they disconnect the phone I'm
going to talk to Y.

Finally, I heard the telltale hiss of distance, and your phone began to ring.
We talked against the clock and the phone company's rates, filling each
other in on the history unfolding in and between our two cities. You say
that thousands of poor families displaced by the hyper-inflation have
camped out on your street, as a sign of protest, in front of the building

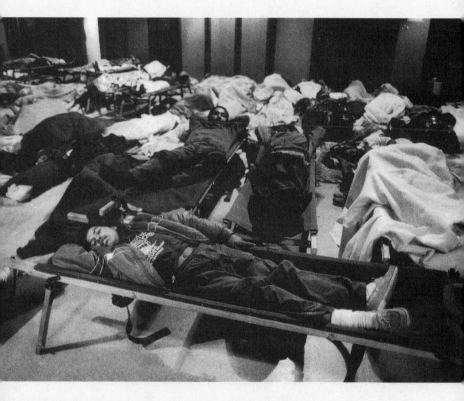

HOMELESS SLEEPING AT LA PLACITA

that houses the Governmental Human Rights Commission. First they had been forced to abandon their rented shacks. Then they erected a shantytown on the edge of one of the city's huge garbage dumps. The authorities descended upon them and gave them half an hour to leave, citing health codes. Within ten minutes the police were dousing gasoline on whatever belongings the poor hadn't been able to carry away. They've spent nearly two weeks camping out on the street in front of the commission, demanding whatever open space is available. Every night, it rains. The children cough with bronchitis.

I give you the latest chapter in the story of La Placita. Olivares has officially left La Placita, and the ministry he established there is being rapidly dismantled. There are now No Loitering signs in the courtyard where hundreds of destitute *jornaleros*, the day laborers who patch, paint, sweep, trim and otherwise keep the city's middle class comfortable, once huddled together each night savoring hot meals. The street vendors have fallen prey to our LAPD (Los Angeles Police Department), which, after Olivares's departure, is suddenly eager to enforce municipal health codes against cooking outdoors (merchants from nearby Olvera Street, a mini tourist mecca, complained that the vendors were unfair competition). The new pastor, one Alberto Vasquez, CMF, has taken down the altar to slain Salvadoran archbishop Oscar Arnulfo Romero, which Olivares had placed in honor of L.A.'s large Salvadoran community. "This was not a sanctuary for refugees," he told the press. "This was a sanctuary for criminals." He added that the Christian Base Communities, crews of activists that Olivares organized, were "being manipulated by communists."

Then you say, Why are we always talking about everything else besides ourselves? How are *you*, tell me, please tell me . . . and we tell each other that our cities should be one.

El Otro Lado

El otro lado,
the other side,
that's where I'm from,
el otro lado,
that's where you're from,
the other side.

Over there! Where it's free,
por allá, ¡sin impuestos!
You know, las calles de
Good Housekeeping oro,
rascacielo-hielo dreams.
Wall Street!
The Street of Walls!
Wall of Neon!
Wall of Mall!
Wall tall!
Ya lo sabes, ahí te espera
todo bien chido . . .
¿Qué what?
Violence?
Never! Not on the streets
of Nuestra Señora la Reina de Los Angeles de Porciúncula!

¡Ay! Pero cómo te deseo,
aquí, desde este lado,
come, cruzá la línea cruda,
vení, vení, come, come,
how I want you on this side!
Let me suck your otherness!
Now, outside of history!
Are you? Are you
outside or inside, playing
the neo-conquistador
and I el suberviso,
a plaything for them?

Deseo-desire deseo-desire deseo-desire
y este deseo acaso real
que se mezcla con quién putas
sabe que verdad
political economic cultural
deseo desire deseo desire deseo
tu saliva extranjera
on this side, but here I
go over there, al otro lado
past your arms to the other
sea and your land
is my water, salty now
with my absence in your
mouth . . .

Baby, where are you now?
¿En Valparaíso?
In Washington DC?
¿En Bogotá?
In Norfolk?
¿En Panamá?
In New Orleans?
¿En Guatemala?

In Santa Fé?
¿En el D.F., guey?
In Las Vegas?
¿En Zacatecas?
In East L.A.?
¿En Chihuahua?
In San Clemente?
¿En Tecate?
In San Diego?
¿Tijuana?
In San Diego?
¿En Tijuana?
In San Diego?
¿En Tijuana?
In San Diego?

Now. At last. Here.
Far from the mortars,
the hungry cities, the false treaties.
Aquí. Al otro lado.

We will finally have each other.
In spectacular contorsion.
¡Deseo! Open me, close me,
here, on this side,
in the exhibition cage
before us and them,
on "Nightline" and "24 Horas."

But tomorrow, it's back
to el otro lado.
Me serving you your breakfast,
your jumbo margarita,
wiping the guacamole off your trousers.

¿Me oyes?
Over there, por allá,
hear me?
Here, me!
This me, this me,
desde este lado,
on this side, este yo
y no el yo del otro,
not your me.
But this me, the one
that wears all the colors
of the continent!

Operadora? Operator?
¿My oyes? Hear me?
No, no te oigo.
Click.

Los Angeles, 1989

Tijuana Burning

April–June 1989

A heavy bass beat—a familiar sound, as though a lowered Toyota pickup had just pulled up next to me at the height of cruising night on Hollywood Boulevard—booms all around me. And light, pounding hearts of lights. This is Avenida Revolución, (or *la Revo*, as it's known to the locals), where discobars like El Vaquero, Tilly's Fifth Ave., Tequila Circo, and Escape! offer to Tijuana's most welcome guests, some thirty million North American tourists each year, the chance to party cheap. To buy cheap. To screw cheap. To don a sombrero that reads "*¡BORRACHO!*" on its broad brim and take a picture sitting astride a burro turned zebra. Or to have a waiter come up behind you at Margarita's Village, jerk your head back in a chokehold, shove a bottle of Gusano Rojo tequila down your throat and shake you like the San Andreas Fault!

I have come here thinking that perhaps by studying this city I will learn something about Los Angeles. After all, isn't L.A. the new Ellis Island, the up-and-coming multicultural capital of the world, the City of the Future? A kind of inverted reflection of L.A. exists, I have been told, in Tijuana, "the cut vein of Latin America that bleeds onto the other side" (as a University of Baja California professor will describe it to me), the city without which L.A. would not be L.A.

The neon burns, the music blasts. The North is here—the disco music. The South is here—the *norteñas* and *cumbias*. And the East—a small but highly visible Chinese population that dates back to the early part of the century, plus plenty of Asian tourists. But what of the people of Tijuana beyond the lurid tourist light of *la Revo*? Over the last few years, a new Tijuana has begun to emerge, a Tijuana that shatters its image as a backyard whorehouse to the States. Its features are being drawn by a group of young local artists whose work reflects the clashing, the melding, the hybridization of culture that is taking place here, virtually invisible to the Northern eye. Today, and for the next few weeks, I will journey a little deeper into Tijuana, a city which is about to celebrate its 100th birthday (on July 11), but which in many ways is just now being born.

A few blocks away from *la Revo*, a complex of bungalows and larger buildings encircles a garden lush enough to make me think of the jungles of Chiapas in southern Mexico. In one bungalow several women artists are working on plaster-of-Paris body molds and canvases to be used in an upcoming installation in San Diego. In another, a journalist is preparing notes for a report to be phoned in to Radio Bilingüe in Fresno. In the underground café and performance space called El Nopal Centenario (The 100-year-old Cactus, so christened in honor of Tijuana's centennial), Felipe Almada, the owner of the complex, contemplates next month's line-up.

In one of the smaller bungalows, I sit cross-legged on the floor and stare at a large canvas entitled *The Legacy of Christophercortéz*. Phantasmagorical figures leap from a bright blue background. A toothless, insectlike priest at the center of the composition shakes the hand of a robot-soldier. A plane bearing the acronyms OPEC and CIA on its fuselage flies over them.

There are drops of blue paint on Hugo Sánchez's leather sandals, on his faded khaki pants, on his naked torso and on his hands. And there is a single drop just below his left eye. "What I'm doing is a kind of graffiti," says the 25-year-old artist, taking a break from work. "A *Tijuagraffiti*, based on my experiences."

This is the second time I've met Hugo. On the first occasion, he'd been in a gloomy, wordless funk over his artistic frustrations. I had only listened as a friend tried to counsel him, and spent a couple of hours trying to understand him via the objects piled chaotically in his studio: back issues of *Art in America*, Arthur Sainer's *The Radical Theater Notebook*, *The Diary of Che Guevara* and heavy, tattered tomes on everyone from the

AZTEC NATION
Tijuana 1989

Mexican muralists Rivera, Siqueiros and Orozco to Jackson Pollock scattered in between, on top and under the trays of oils, acrylics and charcoals. Dozens of sketch pads and canvases filled with convulsively violent images took up nearly all the available wall and floor space in the cramped room.

Since I arrived here, I have heard the word *propuesta* (proposal, or proposition) used by just about everyone who lives in this almost communal environment. The term is equivalent to "manifesto" and takes on almost mythic proportions. Hugo says he wants to develop a new aesthetic, a new identity, "I want to give the child a name." That child is, by turns, Hugo himself, or his fin-de-siècle generation, or the child he longs to father—or the city he lives in.

"Like I was saying," he says, now warming up to the monologue, his hands punctuating the words, "I'm making a kind of graffiti here, with splashes and sprayings and scratches. Women, children and gods all dancing a crazy dance—it's a crossroads, a cross-*commerce*, a cross-*culture*."

A torrent of *propuesta* spills from Hugo's lips, and I'm thinking that I've met the incarnation of Kerouac's Dean Moriarty. But the year is 1989, we're in Tijuana, and to hear Hugo tell it, the survival of an entire hemisphere is at stake. Now he talks of the Spanish Conquest: "the avalanche that crushed our Indian bones"; now of the weight of North America bearing down upon Mexico: "they're a bunch of fascists, we've got to take back what they've taken from us"; now of the border *cholos*, Chicano-style crews of youths who spraypaint their names on the walls of the *barrios populares*, the working-class districts of Tijuana: "heroes in the new struggle for the final liberation"; now about pre-Columbian gods . . . drunken gods, dancing gods, "genius" gods, feathered and unfeathered gods.

"The gods are all around us, *cabrón*, flying in between the skyscrapers and swimming through the sewer lines. The past is roaring into the present, *hermano*, it is whistling in the winds of change! We must listen carefully . . . and ACT!" He gesticulates so intensely that he knocks over the lamp. He giggles, lights a joint, looks at me. I've either found a modern-day Bolívar, I tell myself, or a madman. I'm intrigued by the *propuesta*. But I'm still at a loss as to what, exactly, it is.

In groups of twos and threes throughout the day, the Nopal artists, wearing sunglasses and hung over from an all-night *propuesta* session, have come to sprawl on the green lawn at the center of the complex, where a breeze blows softly though the surrounding peach, yucca, olive and lemon trees. The tranquility is broken only by the occasional jetliner that blasts through the sky close above us, headed north or south. Bottles of tequila and an occasional *caguama* (quart-size beer) are passed around. A battered old beat-box plays the Latin American New Song hits of the sixties and seventies: hope, repression, hope, repression—"I give you a song with my two hands/These two hands that can also kill . . ."

As I get to know my way around El Nopal, I begin to understand that almost everyone here is from somewhere else. Hugo speaks of a childhood in Sonora, and about running away at the age of twelve to Mexico City, where he joined the circus. ("It's true," he says. "The circus!") Then there's María Eraña, a journalist and painter, who was born in Los Angeles (although she's loath to admit it) and arrived here via Mexico City. Local arts organizer and journalist Marco Vinicio González is a member of the growing legion of transplanted *chilangos*, as Mexico City natives are known. Carmela Castrejón, a photographer and "interdisciplinary artist," came down from the North. Like María, Carmela was born *al otro lado*, in San Diego, but she was educated in Tijuana schools. And there's Sydney, a musician from Brazil who grew up in the Amazon, hitched 7,000 miles to the US border, stopped, and decided to explore the town for a few days. That was two years ago.

Not that everyone stays put. Angélica Robles (photographer, painter) and Berta Jottar (video artist, photographer) are locals who continue to work with their colleagues here, but now live on the other side. Gerardo Navarro, a painter and performance artist, fled Tijuana in hope of finding the revolution in Nicaragua and points farther south. And today Hugo tells me that he, too, is on his way south. "Brazil, *hermano*," he smiles. Later, in his room, he shows me a few tourist guides (texts in Portuguese), published in the 1950s: black-and-white stills of Rio beaches, Amazon river scenes, beaming *indígenas*.

"It's one of the most important countries on the continent," he tells me. "I want to nourish myself on the experience of the people there, their plans . . ." Suddenly, he is talking again about the *propuesta*, "this new plan, this new voice, that extends itself all over Latin America, *cabrón*!"

He will put some of this into his last Tijuana project before he leaves, an exhibit at the Casa de la Cultura, the local state-run cultural center. And not just an exhibit—he wants to do a *ritual* (it's performance art, of course, but Hugo will never utter a term used by the *"pinches gringos"*). "I want to conduct a procession through the streets, a *carnaval"* with music, poetry, dance. And most of all, he talks about his *mono*, based on the popular religious tradition of fashioning huge effigies of Judas Iscariot or the devil. It will be a huge plastic-and-Styrofoam *mono*. Which he will burn. Because, Hugo Sánchez says, "I love fire!"

The *propuesta* of this arts community dates back about four years. Up to that time, the Casa de la Cultura, housed in an old brick school building on a hill overlooking downtown Tijuana, had exhibited the usual institutionalized art that the Mexican government tends to sponsor. "There had never been a solid artistic tradition here," says Marco González, the reporter who shuttles back and forth between Tijuana and New York, "much less a vanguard."

The artists who now make up the Nopal community carefully orchestrated a coup d'état by first approaching the conservative administration as innocent volunteers. Soon they were producing events, and after a few political strings were pulled, the Casa fell under their control. They launched a genuine alternative cultural movement: performance pieces—mostly politicized works—and a series of children's workshops replaced the abstract or folkloric works and traditional theater of the previous managers. It wasn't long before Hugo Sánchez arrived with his *rituales*. There was one in which he shaved his head and eyebrows as he ranted, stream-of-consciousness style, about everything from decadent Mexican politics to CIA plots against the revolution. In another, he gathered together a group of small children to help him smash Catholic icons on stage.

The Casa's new look did not please everybody, of course. Catcalls from conservatives ("Extremist elements have taken over the Casa!"), even dissension within the ranks of the new vanguard, led to a counterrevolution. The center today is run by Elsa Arnaiz de Toledo, the Toledos being one of the richest families in Tijuana.

Undaunted, the group transferred its energy to El Nopal, where Felipe Almada offered low rent and support to the suddenly displaced artists. Carrying on the tradition of Latin American political artists of the sixties and seventies who sought to reach, and at the same time were inspired by, the working class, the Nopal community took its work to the streets in increasingly visible artistic–political actions. Early last year, a sixty-foot-long serpent was paraded to the border, along with portable slide projectors that cast images of the war in Nicaragua on walls along the way. As percussionists bashed out an elemental beat, the plastic serpent was set on fire—causing a furor with both Mexican and US border officials, and leading to the arrest of everyone involved. But, recalls Maria Eraña, the Mexican officials "melted" when the artists explained that the act was a protest against the way that Mexicans are treated by the US Border Patrol. "They wound up liking us."

Then there was last year's action commemorating the army massacre of Mexican university students at Tlatelolco on October 2, 1968. At Santa Cecilia Plaza near the border, murals were thrown up, poems read, and "border punk" band Mercado Negro (Black Market) played while a cardboard replica of an army tank, equipped with a machinegun-fire soundtrack, plowed incessantly into the crowd. Finally, a group of punks turned on it and smashed it to pieces. Afterward the Nopal artists placed dozens of lit candles around the destroyed tank, and a moment of silence was held.

"For me, the aim of the work in the streets is to engage in a direct dialogue with people," Carmela Castrejón tells me. "The work is for them, not for the galleries." Immediately, I think back to my poet colleagues in El Salvador, and waves of nostalgia wash over me. But what fascinates me most about all of this is the synthesis of the ideals of the sixties generation and the aesthetic breakthroughs of later years. It seems that the child that Hugo is obsessed with naming is already developing a personality.

Perhaps the most essential aspect of Tijuana's identity is its own identity crisis. After all, Tijuana owes its very existence to cultural Others, especially North American Others. Yes, there were once Native Americans here who loosely gravitated around the San Diego Mission established by Father Junipero Serra in 1769. But in 1848, the treaty of Guadalupe Hidalgo split California and, according to Rubén Vizcaíno, a philosophy professor at the University of Baja California and an expert on Tijuana, "the *Tijuanenses* lost their identity." Since then, he says, "The historical essence of Tijuana has been tourism."

Hugo has insisted on this pilgrimage to the venerable professor ("The oracle on the mountain"), and listens raptly. Vizcaíno, a cantankerous man in his seventies who, judging by his short, fat tie, yellowed shirt and suspenders, probably hasn't bought a new suit since the fifties, leans back in his chair at his university library office, surrounded by piles of books and papers. As late as 1900, he tells me, Tijuana was still but a speck on the map, a *ranchito* with an unimpressive population of 242. It was the construction of military bases in San Diego, along with Prohibition, that established Tijuana's legend as an "anything goes" town, built by North Americans along with Mexicans with a keen business sense and no scruples about national pride. The architecture of *la Revo* today—a mishmash of Deco, Neo-Colonial and Bauhaus—tells that story.

Then came the tourists, says Vizcaíno, "looking for *their* identity." The *gringos* fancy themselves "supermen, leaders of the Free World, technological gods. They see Third World poverty—the skinny dogs, the people begging, the *indígenas* kneeling before them—and they prove to themselves that they are great. Get it?" ("Yes! Yes! Yes!" cries Hugo, rocking back and forth in his chair.)

By 1930, the population was just under 12,000. Soon the waves of immigration from the South rolled, first after the Mexican Revolution and the later Cristero War, then as a result of the US wartime worker ("*bracero*") programs of the forties. But the wave turned back on itself and surged southward again with the massive deportations of Mexican nationals after the Korean War. The population in 1950: 60,000. In the mid-sixties, the Mexican government, seeking foreign investment, established the *maquiladora* system, foreign-owned assembly plants taking advantage of the country's cheap labor market. Because most people used Tijuana as a conduit for arriving in the States, the city's population was extremely unstable. But each wave headed north or south deposited more and more permanent residents.

The prospects of work, in Tijuana and in the North, have continued to attract new generations of immigrants from the South. By 1980, the population had swelled to upwards of 450,000, according to conservative Mexican estimates. Following the wars in Central America, and the Mexican economic crisis of the early eighties, the population is now believed to be anywhere from one and a half million to two million.

Vizcaíno, like Hugo, has a mission—to establish Tijuana's "identity." But fifty million tourists a year make it difficult, as do the many thousands of TV sets that tune in nightly to the transmissions from San Diego and points north. And then there are the kids who seek only to imitate the latest Northern fads—they even do their shopping *al otro lado*! As for those who lobby for a cultural eclecticism, who toy with the idea of melting the border down . . . for Vizcaíno, that's neither possible nor desirable. "What's desirable is that one have an identity." A Latin American identity.

In the yard at El Nopal, Hugo, wearing an orange–red sweatshirt, works on his *mono* under a funereal gray sky (typical June weather, just like L.A.). Today he's fuming over his show at the Casa de la Cultura, which is only a few days away. The directors of the center are already giving him problems, he tells me. The millionaire's daughter doesn't want him burning anything. She's also worried about Mercado Negro, whom Hugo has enlisted for the *ritual*, bringing in their punk anarchy. "I told her that her job is to support local artists. She told me not to raise my voice." Hugo now calls the center the "Casa de la Caca."

He straddles the bulging Styrofoam, which he has shaped with chicken wire and is now wrapping in brightly colored plastic. Two tall bamboo poles lie on the grass next to the *mono*. They will form the cross with which Hugo will carry it up to the Casa.

"This is the prodigal son, the one that burns," he tells me. "He burns all the time, burning inside his own skin, you know, in his profound desire to be born again, to bathe in blood and wine and in the struggle . . ."

It sounds like scripted dialogue. Or poetry. (Or both.) But there is no script. I don't have to ask questions—the torrent continues without my prompting. Once more, however, I ask him to define the *propuesta*. His *mono* represents what? He tightens the chicken wire. He pushes in the Styrofoam here and it pops out over there.

"A multiple ideology," says Hugo. "I believe in the ideology of Marx and

Lenin. I was a Catholic, and then I was a Mason, then a Protestant. Then a Stoic, then an anarchist, and finally a fuck-it-all-ist. There've been all these changes, mixed with memories and experiences . . ." He grabs the *mono*'s arm and begins to dance with it as if to a *norteña* rhythm.

"And I'm always asking myself about history. History! HISTORY! All those heroes—Zapata, Orozco, Nietzsche, Christ, Marx, Guillén, Artaud, Fuentes, Heraclitus, Rulfo, Brecht, Hesse, Gibran—those personages, those dates and those times. Because through them, through their emotion, we're going to find the future . . ."

The rumbling of a jet passing overhead unseen in the fog grows louder and louder until his voice is drowned out. He continues to pinch at the Styrofoam, twist the chicken wire.

"We are revolutionaries, Catholics, Arabs, forgotten ones, exiled ones, in Tijuana," he says after the jet has passed, and he suddenly stops working the *mono*. "Everything is multiple. We're rained on by everything, soaked to the skin. There's this rain, man. There's a rain that I see, a rain of fire and water, of seas and clouds, it rains rains rains rains rains, a living rain that nourishes itself on hope, that becomes little drops of faith."

Legs, shoulders, faces, breasts lie on top of the table. A huge papier-mâché skull sits on a chair. Nearby, Carmela Castrejón and María Eraña work side by side on paintings that feature bikinied blondes, the kind you see in Pepsi beach commercials. When Hugo, Marco and I enter—we'll serve as male models for more papier-mâché body parts—it is the first time since I arrived that the men and women of El Nopal have come together in a work setting.

The women's installation is for the Sushi Performance Gallery in San Diego. The concept originated from a critique of the last Tijuana show there, in which not a single woman artist participated. This, I am told, is par for the course. "We used to help the men with their performances and exhibitions," says María Eraña. "But now that we have an exhibit, they just watch from a distance."

Hugo and Marco ask questions. Lots of them. "What exactly is the nature of your collaboration?" "Why don't you want to work with us?" "Is there some fundamental difference between the way you work and the way we do?"

The women spend much of their time rejecting the male preconceptions

PERFORMANCE
Tijuana 1989

about their work. "No, we are not 'feminists.' Don't label us with North American terminology!" "We just felt like working together—stop trying to impose your interpretations on us." "But there are differences. Why is your work so violent?" "Yes, Hugo, why are you always burning things?"

After Marco's face has been greased with Vaseline, his mouth is sealed shut with a layer of hot plaster of Paris. A few minutes later, Hugo has been stripped down to his bikini shorts and lies in a pose à la *Playgirl*. His mouth and body are covered, too. The discussion with the men is, apparently, over.

María and Carmela, now joined by Angélica Robles, begin work on new drawings depicting different stereotypes—wholesome, motherly Latinas, exotic dancers ("We're bombarded with these images daily"), all culled from B-flicks and tabloids. One piece, they tell me, will be the "Genealogical Tree," filled out with the Latina heroines—Frida Kahlo, María Sabina, Rosario Castellanos, Sor Juana Inez de la Cruz—that are usually missing from the Mexican history told by the macho males.

The body parts, Carmela tells me, will take up a whole wall at the gallery. "It'll be a huge chasm full of bodies," she says, her hair splattered with plaster of Paris and her eyes puffy—she's been working day and night. "It represents the tension between Mexico and the United States, particularly how the North interprets the South." This is one thing the male and female artists of El Nopal have in common: classic, unbridled anti-Americanism.

"When I see the Marines come down here and get drunk, I feel this hatred," María says. "When I see them toss money at the poor children, I feel an irrepressible anger."

"They just come down to use us," says Angélica.

"I feel nausea when I see them," says Carmela, as she slaps more hot plaster of Paris on Hugo's body. "I just wish I could erase them."

One night, I accompany the Nopal artists on an outing to several nightclubs. Rather than enter the mammoth, strobe-lit disco bars, the crew heads straight for one of its favorite local hangouts, La Estrella, a working-class club barely half a block from *la Revo*. Here, everyone is dancing to a *cumbia*, not a disco beat. The *cumbia*, with its two-chord arrangements and horse-trot rhythm, is a *campesino* tradition from the south of Mexico, but here it is in urbanized Tijuana, part of the cultural baggage of the millions of Southerners who have come north seeking work.

Every inch of the dance floor is taken by couples. Hundreds of other men and women sit on the surrounding benches. For many of the men, who are from Oaxaca, Michoacán, Guerrero and other southern and western Mexican states, La Estrella is the last stop before they "bleed" onto the other side. Some are bleary-eyed or have passed out face down on the wooden tables. Others stare forlornly at the dance floor, where an occasional buxom, dressed-to-kill transsexual draws their attention by dancing before them in an extremely low-cut dress.

For most of the women here, it is a different story. They live in Tijuana (though, like the men, they are usually from the South), and most have jobs at the *maquiladoras*. Typical profile: early twenties, single, ten-hour workdays (six days a week), $40 weekly income. They work for Sanyo or Samsung, for Gamesa (the Mexican food conglomerate) and Ericson Yachts Inc., in the nearby Ciudad Industrial, where the real-estate signs are in Spanish, English and Japanese, and where dirt-cheap 99-year leases on residential and industrial properties are the norm.

"La Estrella is becoming an alternative hangout," jokes Marco González. Why? "This is *rasquachismo*," he says: an aesthetic he describes as working class, kitschy, imperfect, improvised, erotic, violent . . . in short, it is *cultura popular*, where the Nopal artists leave *la Revo* behind, cross class lines and are with *el pueblo*, the working-class heroes. Hugo, uncomfortable perhaps with this somewhat romantic notion, suddenly turns cynical. "It's here that we masturbate to our working-class fantasies," he says.

Later, at Los Esquipales, one of Tijuana's premier discobars for young, upscale gays and lesbians, a transvestite is lip-synching to one of the melodramatic disco ballads of Mexican pop star Daniela Romo. The next *trasvesti* does Annie Lennox. "This is just Barbie culture," says Marco González disdainfully.

The next act is an unexpected show-stopper. A portly, mustachioed man—size twelve feet, overalls—waddles onto the stage. His wig spills silky black hair down his back. The disco pulse fades, a *cumbia* comes on, and the crowd goes wild. Young man after young man leaps up to the stage to stuff a bill in the front pocket of the man's overalls, and to steal a kiss.

Marco and the others are overjoyed. "This," he proclaims triumphantly, "is the *response* to Barbie culture!"

The sun wants to break through the clouds today, almost does. Enough light cuts through the gray curtain for our figures to make shadows in the garden. Hugo is up before everyone else. Tonight his exhibit opens and the *mono* will burn. Steadily, Hugo's ideas for the *ritual* have grown more complex. Now he wants everyone at El Nopal to participate, a grand procession of death and love and violence and eroticism down the streets and right up to the Casa de la Cultura. "*¡Un carnaval, hermano!*"

Hugo seems distracted this morning, though, as he gathers up the murals, drawings and other materials for the trip to the center. He's thinking about Brazil. He's no longer sure whether he wants to go south. There have been new *propuestas*, right here among his colleagues in Tijuana. A musician friend has suggested that they tour Mexico, a kind of traveling minstrel–*ritual* show, from the great cities like Zacatecas and Mexico City to the outlying areas of Oaxaca and Chiapas. "I don't know whether or not I should postpone the Brazil trip," he says, his hands gesturing intensely in front of his Che Guevara T-shirt. He strikes a match and stares at the flame until it's on the verge of burning his fingers, before finally lighting a cigarette. "I don't know what to do, *hermano*," he says, exhaling smoke. "I don't know what to do."

The procession stops traffic along the avenue that leads to the Casa. Children and adults stare wide-eyed from their cars or from the sidewalks as Hugo Sánchez, back glistening with sweat, face contorted in pain, struggles under the weight of the huge cross that carries the *mono*. Behind him a ragtag crew of drummers pounds away on assorted skins. Carmela, María, Berta and Angélica bear aloft papier-mâché skeletons and skulls, whirling about like gypsies. Bringing up the rear, traipsing along merrily atop a pair of stilts, is performance artist Elia Arce, who has come from L.A. especially for the procession, wearing a huge mask representing Roque Dalton, the martyred Salvadoran poet–revolutionary. Around her a group of *barrio* children are clutching sheets

BURNING THE MONO

torn from a book by Roque, declaiming fragments of poems about war and love.

Hugo's Passion is all too real. Six flights of stairs wind their way up to the Casa, which is perched atop a hill that gives a panoramic view of Tijuana, the border and *el otro lado*. Hugo takes each step slowly, groaning, shutting his eyes against the pain. Above us, the heavens have cleared completely for the first time since I've arrived. A full moon shines down upon us, and we climb, slowly but steadily, ever higher.

On the last flight of stairs, Hugo stumbles and falls face flat onto the concrete. The drummers and the children surround him, but he yells that he wants to be left alone. "The child must complete his mission," he says, gasping for breath, completely immersed in his quest. Halfway up that final flight he stops again, his legs on the verge of buckling. The procession behind him waits in silence. Hugo stares up at the full moon as a fresh breeze cools down the assembled followers.

Minutes later, we storm the Casa, packing the entryway where the drumming reaches a deafening pitch and Roque and the *mono* dance together frenetically. All around us on the walls are Hugo's works, some of them thirty feet long, iconographic maps of horror and redemption, the never-ending Latin American saga.

Rushing outside the Casa, Hugo props up the crucified monster and splashes it with gasoline. About one hundred people gather around the effigy in the dusk. The percussionists again begin a primitive rhythm, while Hugo circles the *mono* with fists clenched, chanting hoarsely in a Caribbean patois: "*Serembehhhhhhhbeh! Yarombohhhhhh!*" For one last time, he stops and stares at his "son", and then ignites it with a cigarette lighter.

The eruption of flame sends out a blast of heat and light that causes the crowd to scatter. The plastic burns bright, and quickly. Each time the fire begins to die down, Hugo, still circling and chanting, pours more gasoline onto it, until the foam and plastic are gone, leaving only the naked chickenwire frame glowing red. He kicks the skeleton a couple of times. Showers of sparks leap toward the moon.

Como le vamos a poner al niño? How are we going to name the child?

Tonight, Hugo is back on the downtown streets of Tijuana, seeking "identity." Or maybe just wanting to get drunk. In any case, we're drawn to *la Revo*'s flame. U2's "Pride (In the Name of Love)" is playing on one side of the street as the Miami Sound Machine pumps away on the other, while a block away *cumbias* abound.

Propuestas. The happening at the Casa was just the beginning. Hugo wants to do more *rituales*. In front of the lines of people waiting for the buses. In the parks. On the border. Before crowds. Huge crowds. Five thousand people. Here, in Mexico City, in Los Angeles, in Rio de Janeiro. "I want to burn, man. I want to *burn*."

We walk slowly up and down *la Revo* . . . *gringos*, border *cholos*, Japanese tourists . . . Hugo can't figure out where to go tonight. He wants to show me the real Tijuana. First, it's a bar where the disco pulses and a naked woman writhes under the red spotlight on stage. She leans down before a tourist, who buries his face in her breasts. On the next block, a young longhair croons pop songs in English to the Americanized Tijuana bourgeoisie. That's not it either. Then we're out on the street again, passing by the taco stands next to the hotdog stands, the *indígenas* proffering their Guatemalan-style "friendship bracelets" and lizards of colored foam.

And Brazil? It's hard to leave, Hugo admits. There's so much to do here, right on the border. The child needs a name.

L.A. Journal (V)

September 1990

Going through one of my late Mexican grandparents' scrapbooks, I come across a black-and-white glossy. My grandmother is decked out in classic Spanish Romantic attire, a chiffon crown in the style of the nineteenth century on her head and trailing down her back, a ruffled, floor-length dress, white flowers in her hair. Similarly, my grandfather's silk-trim vest and black trousers, with a dark kerchief spilling out from the left pocket, loosely approximate a Spanish don. My grandparents are both standing, cradling their guitars and holding down a D-7 in the first position. Seated to their right at a dinner table is a white gentleman in an expensive, bureaucratic–conservative suit. He is smiling. He is also holding a gun. It looks like a real standard police issue of the period. The gun is pointed at my grandparents. This is a funny joke. My grandmother smiles effusively, with those perfect teeth of hers (cavityless her entire life), and my grandfather also plays along—smiling as he cowers away from the pistol.

The Paris Inn, where my grandparents played Mexican *ranchera* music for the city's elite, was a hot night spot throughout the 1940s. As I leaf through the photo album stuffed with dozens of photos of my grand-parents entertaining, I suddenly imagine myself walking into the Paris Inn dressed in a sleeveless T-shirt and khakis, cool shades hiding my eyes, a crucifix dangling from my left earlobe. I ignore the maitre d' and his astonished look, sit down at a table and start snapping bread sticks, making a pile of crumbs over the white tablecloth. A nervous waiter comes over, backed up by a posse of two Mexican busboys. "*¡Ahórale!*" I

GRANDPARENTS
The Paris Inn c. 1929

THE PARIS INN
c. 1946

say, leaning back as far as possible, à la El Pachuco in Luis Valdez's *Zoot Suit*. "For starters, how about some chips and salsa? *Y luego, tres tacos de carne asada, dos de lengua, y uno de carnitas. Y luego, maestro, me trae dos pupusas, una revuelta y una de queso. Ah! Y no se le olvide una Tecate bien heladita con limoncito y sal. He dicho.*" I clap my hands and wave them off. The customers are all looking my way—the bureaucrat with the gun is giving me a real hard look. And my grandparents, they pretend they don't know me, can you believe it? But, maybe they just don't recognize me dressed like a *cholo*. Come to think of it, my grandmother would probably burst into tears if she *did* recognize me, so I make like I don't know them either . . .

. . . but over by the bar there's Humphrey, I mean Rick, and his watery and my red eyes lock. The slightest smile cracks those perpetually pouting lips, and with a slight nod of the head he motions over to the back exit. The door is open. I can see the silver cargo plane out on the rain-glazed runway, its propellers starting to turn over. I make a run for it. "Get away from that phone!" I hear Rick yell at the bureaucrat, who's dialling the LAPD from the phone at the front desk. The shots ring out behind me as I bound out onto the runway, where Y is waiting, enshrouded by the fog . . .

Going Up in L.A.

Los Angeles, April 1989

The stain on the old couch that sits in the empty lot has already turned brown, a dark flower spread out upon the grimy fabric. Although it's a school day and only 10:30 in the morning, about a dozen teenagers stand about, passing around a quart of Colt 45 Malt Liquor. Some of the faces show fear; others are hardened into stony stares. "We know who did it, but we're not going to tell you," says one of the younger boys. His hair is cropped stubby short, and he wears dark jeans and a plain T-shirt. "We're not going to spell it out, but you can pretty much guess what's going to happen tonight."

At approximately seven o'clock the previous evening, these kids had been seated on or standing around the couch. Among the group was Prime, a seventeen-year-old homeboy. They'd all been "kickin' it"—drinking and talking to the accompaniment of a ghettoblaster alternately pumping out hip-hop and oldies—when a car pulled up to the curb below, and two figures climbed up the hill in the darkness. "Where you from?" one of them yelled from a distance of about ten feet. A moment later, several rounds exploded from a shotgun and a .45. Prime and another boy fell in the hail of bullets, and lay bleeding on the couch.

We walk around to the side of one of the dilapidated stucco bungalows that crown the hill. A wall displays the local gang's roster—hundreds of names spraypainted in furious, spidery lettering. Someone points to the "R.I.P." section: more than a dozen names. "Rest In Power," mumbles one of the boys. Nobody is sure whether the next name to go up on the wall will be Prime's.

PRIME

A few days earlier, Prime was sitting in his family's living room, which doubles as a bedroom, in a neighborhood not far from the empty lot. It is a crime-ridden area to be sure, dominated by one of the city's oldest Latino gangs. This is where Prime grew up, and where his two unemployed parents try to scrape by on welfare.

Although Prime admitted that he'd been "in the wrong place at the wrong time" on more than one occasion, he saw himself less as a gangster, more as a "writer" (as graffiti artists call themselves), one of the best-known among the city's thousands of young, spraycan-wielding "bombers."

Prime shook hands gingerly that day. His right hand still bore the chalky plaster stains from a cast that had been removed the day before, the bones in his right—and writing—hand having been broken in a fist fight.

As soon as I entered the room, he began to show off his canvases. After years of doing complex, colorful works on walls across the city, Prime had begun experimenting with acrylics, airbrush, oils, washes. It was Valentine's Day, and he'd done a piece for his girlfriend—a brightly colored Cupid surrounded by soft pink roses, with a dedication that read, "José and Nery, *por vida*." He pointed to a larger work dominated by grays, blacks and silvers, titled *Dazed and Confused*, an ambitious circular composition centered on a pair of dice that become a large syringe, then a huddled, shadowy figure and, finally, a large, wicked-looking skull.

Prime sat down on the sagging bed, the plaster wall behind him bulging with cracked paint. At the age of eight, he tells me, he snatched his sister's goldfleck hairspray and wrote "Little Joe, 18 Street" in the back yard. Soon afterward his initials were "up" in the neighborhood alleys.

"I never got really crazy," he told me. But as gang violence in the inner city increased dramatically in the mid-1980s, he was busted for various misdemeanors, including "vandalism" (i.e., spraypainting), and he once almost did time for armed robbery. It wasn't until about 1984 that Prime graduated from gang-writing to more original and complex forms of graffiti. He developed a style that set him apart from other graffiti artists, working closely with several colleagues in the K2S–STN ("Kill To Succeed–Second To None") crew, one of the first to appear on the city's Eastside.

By last Valentine's Day, Prime could look back on it all and vow that it was the art that really mattered in his life. And, as he brought out photo albums stuffed with color photographs of graffiti works he'd done over the years, he told me he'd enrolled in art classes at the East L.A. Occupational Center. He spoke to me of a future without drive-by shootings, overdoses or girls pregnant at fifteen. "I want to have a big lot when I grow older," he said, leaning forward, a small gold crucifix swinging in front of his dark blue sweatshirt. "It'll have big, long, movable walls. I'll put canvases up, and have kids and artists there, have it be like a big maze of art. Then, with the money I make in one day, I'll buy some more canvas and change the maze . . ."

By 1984, movies like *Wild Style, Beat Street* and *Breakin'* had apprised L.A. teenagers of the graffiti writing explosion that had taken place in the Bronx, where a complex, multicolored graffiti known as "wildstyle" had evolved in the late 1970s and early 1980s. Behind its New York counterparts by several years, L.A. created its own distinct scene. In New York, most of the work had been painted onto the sides of subway cars. L.A.'s answer was to "bomb" the freeways.

L.A. writers had a rich history to draw upon. Graffiti had been around since the World War Two era Pachucos (the first style-conscious Latino gangs, who incorporated Old English lettering into their "tags," or nicknames); the East L.A. mural artists of the sixties, with their close ties to Mexican muralism, were a local artistic and political institution. The city was ripe for a new public-art explosion.

The city's first graffiti "crew" was the L.A. Bomb Squad, whose membership consisted almost exclusively of Latino youths from the *barrios* of Pico-Union and East L.A. Soon, however, the movement spread west, south and north, to include teens from other impoverished neighborhoods and from the middle-class suburbs as well.

And so the L.A. version of hip-hop graffiti was born. Many of the more aesthetically developed works (known as "pieces", short for "master-pieces") were done in hidden-away places like the Belmont Tunnel, an old, fenced-off trolley stop near Belmont High School. There were also more daring exploits. Simple tags and "throw-ups" (two-color tags) went up on buses, benches, sidewalks, street lights, stop signs, anywhere that was highly visible to the public. Competition as to who could top whom in originality and quantity was intense.

THE BELMONT TUNNEL

The glory days of the nascent L.A. scene came in 1984, when a youth club named Radio-Tron opened its doors. "It was a cultural center where people could go practice breaking and drawing," recalls Moda (the tag is Spanish for "fashion"), a founding member of the Bomb Squad. Housed in a building in the Westlake *barrio* near MacArthur Park, Radio-Tron was akin to an established artist's studio, a haven from the streets where writers always ran the risk of a bust. Soon, every inch of the site was covered with tags and pieces. "All the guys I knew were being thrown in jail or getting killed," says Primo D, also of the Bomb Squad. "Radio-Tron was an alternative."

The center's curriculum, according to founder and director Carmelo Alvarez, a longtime inner-city youth activist, included deejaying, scratch and rap, and "advanced graffiti." "I just took what they had and structured it." But the experiment didn't last long. Wrangles with the city (Alvarez balked when the Department of Parks and Recreation made a move to take over the center), as well as a Fire Marshall's citation (for storage of "hazardous chemicals"—aerosol cans), led to its being closed. "When Radio-Tron shut down, everybody started getting into the gang thing," says Primo D. "There was nothing else to do."

Not long after the Bomb Squad's tags and cartoonlike "characters" first appeared in the downtown area, a group of mostly middle-class Anglo Westside teens took note and founded WCA (West Coast Artists), soon the biggest crew in the city with an active membership of about thirty-five, plus a subsidiary crew (BC, or Beyond Control) of a dozen or so. Today, on any given weekend morning, you can see WCA at work, along with other Westside crews like KSN (Kings Stop at Nothing), at one of their favorite spots, the Motor Yard in West Los Angeles.

Everything in the yard, including the rails, the ties, the torched wrecks of cars, has been tagged, pieced, bombed—as the writers say, "terrorized." The thousands of discarded spraycans testify to the countless generations of pieces that have gone up, one on top of another, on the half-mile stretch of concrete retaining wall that flanks the railroad tracks.

Carrying in dozens of Krylon spraycans in backpacks or milk crates, the crews usually arrive early in the day and work alongside the railroad tracks that run parallel to the Santa Monica freeway near National Boulevard. A box will invariably be blasting Eazy E's "Boys-N-the-Hood" or Boogie Down Production's "My Philosophy" as the writers, ranging in age from six to their early twenties, fish sketches out of their back pockets, the cans, press down customized nozzles ("fat tips" culled from small Testor's spraycans, which allow for a thicker, smoother line) and begin the sweeping rhythmic motions that trace the skeleton of a new piece.

Phoe of BC, a wiry, clean-cut teenager of Hawaiian–Filipino ancestry, is there one weekend, wearing a dark blue baseball cap embroidered with the name of his crew. His tag, he tells me, is an intentional misspelling of "foe," which, according to him, means "society's enemy." He works on a three-dimensional wildstyle piece that is typical of Westside work. The edges of the letters are sharp as shards of glass, but serif-like cuts and arrows make the composition virtually unreadable to the untrained eye.

"Writing is, like, a different community," says Phoe, yelling to be heard over the freeway roar that almost drowns out his high-pitched voice. "It's communication with other writers throughout the city." Wherever he goes ("even when I go out to dinner with my parents"), the tools of the trade—markers or spraycans—are at his disposal.

As with many Westside writers, Phoe's response to the city's anti-graffiti forces, or to those sympathetic adults who encourage him to professionalize his talent, is lackadaisical. "Yeah, yeah, yeah. They're telling me to go out and sign up for scholarships and art classes, and get paid for writing, and I'm, like, well, I don't really need the money because I work." Yet some WCA writers do take "legal" jobs now and then, pounding the streets in search of sympathetic business owners who'll pay them to paint storefront signs and the like. Risk, one of WCA's premier writers, recently did backgrounds for a Michael Jackson video.

Still, there's an allure to the "illegal" work. And, since most writers lack studio space, sites like the Motor Yard are indispensable. "They just don't understand," says Ash, another respected WCA writer. "We need this place to paint, or else we're going to bomb the streets more, straight up."

Although a few Westside writers are friendly with their Eastside counterparts, interaction between the two groups is limited. Indeed, the

NBC – NEVER BEEN CAUGHT

rivalry between WCA and K2S–STN dates back to the origins of the L.A. writing scene. Like breakdancers, writers "battle" each other. The spoils of victory may include several dozen spraycans, or the appropriation of a writer's tag.

As soon as WCA and K2S–STN each became aware of the other, the stage was set for the East–West battle, which took place at the Belmont Tunnel in 1985. WCA went up with the bigger production in their trademark flashy style, featuring a pastel-yellow/clover-green/pastel-aqua, black-outlined, white-highlighted, hot-pink-and-avocado-bordered piece by Risk. Next to it was a character by fellow writer Cooz, of a Japanese-animation-style buxom woman wearing shiny wraparound shield glasses, a cascade of auburn hair spilling over her shoulders.

K2S–STN countered with a shocker from Prime. Employing an abstract, futuristic style, he wrote his tag with an altered color scheme and composition: triangles and squares of hot pink, white, true blue and baby blue produced a new kind of three-dimensional effect. Next to it he drew a robot character he'd found in a comix mag.

Some West Coast writers congratulated Prime afterward in an apparent admission of defeat. By the next morning, however, all of the WCA productions, as well as a substantial part of Prime's, had been "dissed" (painted over) by unknown writers, and the bad blood began. To this day, some WCA writers maintain that Prime was the culprit, although he always denied the allegation.

There are substantial stylistic differences between East and West Los Angeles writers. WCA writers are sensitive to the charge that they are "biting" (the writer's term for plagiarism) New York styles. "We took the New York styles and made them into our own style," says Wisk, the crew's most prolific writer, a little defensively. Using thin letters with stylized swirls and blends of color accented with arrows and sparkles, West Coast's work often achieves a slick magazine look—the New York stamp is unmistakable. K2S–STN, on the other hand, while sometimes drawing on the same influences, produces more readable block- or bubblelike letters that echo old gang-writing styles updated with the wildstyle. The result is aesthetically analogous to the split between the Anglo and ethnic art worlds of the 1960s and 1970s—playful abstraction on the one hand, Socialist Realism-flavored work on the other.

K2S–STN

Kill To Succeed—Second To None

But the stylistic differences between the two groups hide deeper tensions. The Eastside writers, who lay claim to being the original Los Angeles bombers, feel that WCA has received a disproportionate share of media attention, including articles in the *Los Angeles Times* that have largely ignored the Eastside writers in favor of Westsiders.

"It was only when white people started doing graffiti that they said it was art," Prime once said bitterly. "We were doing it before them, but [the media] were blaming us for vandalism." These sentiments are echoed by most Eastside writers, and their resentment is obviously both class- and race-based.

"Most of the West Coast writers are from middle-class families," says Moda of the original L.A. Bomb Squad. "On this side of town, you're faced with the gang problem and graffiti at the same time. It affects the writers from poor neighborhoods: because they have the distraction of gangs, they might not be able to pursue it all the way. Like Prime—he's stuck between gangs and graffiti."

Prime's father approaches the bed slowly. An oxygen mask all but hides the son's incipient beard and mustache. Dried blood is still encrusted on his forehead and temples. The father takes his son's bloody hand into his own, leans down and whispers something into his ear. Prime tries to speak, but the words are mumbled, delirious. His father lifts back the white sheet and peers at Prime's right arm, swathed in bandages. After two major operations, the doctors are finally willing to predict that Prime is going to make it.

Over the next few days, Prime's fellow writers will visit his bedside in an endless procession. Among them is Duke, twenty years old, a native of Guatemala and a seven-year writing veteran of K2S–STN. Like Prime, Duke has been involved in gangsterism. When he heard the news about the shooting, his first impulse was "to go out and take care of shit," but he checked himself. "The art took me out of the trip," says Duke, who is dressed in his trademark smoke-gray jeans, his boyish face showing a spotty beard. "It helped me to look at this world in a more positive sense."

Initiated into gangs at an early age, Duke says his first spraycan escapade involved simple tagging. But after some heavy violence on the streets—he was once tied to a car bumper by rival gang members and dragged for two blocks—he decided to try to "clean up his act." When the first wave of graffiti art hit L.A., he began devoting more and more of his time to piecing.

"I wanted to kick back," Duke says of the early days of graffiti. At that time, when he was in tenth grade, "jungle football" clubs were sprouting up all over the inner city. The emphasis at first was on sports, but soon fights were breaking out between the rival groups. Then guns were brandished, and the club Duke had helped to organize quickly became one of the largest gangs in the Pico-Union area, a *barrio* that is home to over a quarter of a million central Americans.

Early one morning in October 1985, a shotgun blast tore Duke's stomach open as he was walking to school. The doctors later told him it was a miracle that he had survived. Then came family problems and a difficult separation from his girlfriend. He gave up writing for months and found himself at a crossroads, uncertain as to which path to follow. But today he's back in the writing scene, and serious about moving up from the streets to a "legal" career by painting storefront signs and doing everything he can to set up his own art studio at home.

Prime, like Duke, had begun to distance himself from the gang world before he was shot. "He wasn't the kind to go out and say, 'Let's take care of these dudes,'" says Duke after visiting Prime one day. "Thank God he's not gone. And I hope he never goes." Like Geo, who was shot for yelling out the wrong gang name when they asked him, "Where you from?" Or Sine, who was stabbed when he tried to defend a younger kid from a gangster wielding a switchblade. Or Risko, who died in a car that tumbled off a Harbor Freeway overpass as he and another friend fled from the police after a gang outing. All were writers associated with K2S–STN.

Veterans of the writing scene estimate that at any given time there are probably several hundred full-fledged writers at work in Los Angeles. But one must add to this figure the hundreds, perhaps thousands of teens who are bombing the city with single-color tags, the bane of the Rapid Transit District and other city agencies. "There are so many people into tagging, and that's what's messing it up for the people who do art," says Cash, a

K2S–STN veteran. "Tags, all they do is destroy, make the city look ugly. The art beautifies the walls that have been tagged up."

On the other hand, there is no doubt that straight-out vandalism is part of the appeal, especially for the younger, or "toy," writers. On a recent Friday ("Ditching Day") morning, the Panic Zone, East L.A.'s best-known writing yard, was crawling with up-and-coming writers, most of them of junior high school age, and their crew names alone—KCC (Kids Committing Crime) and CIA (Criminals In Action)—tell the story. With a ravenous hunger for recognition, they announce their names: POSES, KORE, MICRO, MIST, ERGER, SED, SOEWHAT, DEVO, SKOE, DEES, STINGER, BEAST, DEFEAT, KINE, SETO. The selection of a tag is the all-important first step in establishing the writer's originality (hence the purposeful misspellings). Most of the tags deliberately cultivate either a dark, brooding image—DOOM, DREAD, DYE—or conjure a notion of hip-hop "badness"—REGENT, PRIME, SLICK.

The young writers at the Panic Zone are rabid taggers. "We all write on 'em all," proclaims one writer whose voice hasn't changed yet, pointing at the buses lined up at the Rapid Transit District maintenance yard, which lies only about fifty yards from the northernmost end of the Panic Zone. Why? "To get up, be known!" he says, and all the other writers nod eagerly.

Government agencies in Los Angeles County spend some $150 million annually in the war against graffiti. Sandblasters are available for heavy-duty "buffing" across the city, and a city-run warehouse doles out free paint to any citizen who asks for it. (30,000 gallons, enough to cover 6 million square feet of graffiti, have been given away since 1986.) A legal offensive is also in the works. Daniel Ramos, a.k.a. Chaka, probably the most prolific writer in the history of graffiti (some 10,000 tags up and down the state), was busted by the LAPD and the City Attorney threw the proverbial book at him. He languished in jail for months and was recently assigned to a special reformatory "boot camp." Anti-graffiti forces, springing from well-to-do and generally conservative home-owners' associations nationwide, have lobbied for special anti-graffiti legis-lation—a ban on the sale of spraycans, for example.

"We're really deterring them," says LAPD spokesperson William

KINGS STOP AT NOTHING

Medina, who coordinates a neighborhood cleanup effort in the Rampart *barrio* area of L.A. For the LAPD, even the elaborate pieces that have gone up at the various "yards" around town are considered illegal. "We view it as graffiti," says Medina. "The only things we don't consider illegal are [city-] organized and approved murals."

Community meetings focusing on graffiti typically draw standing-room-only audiences. Responding to an increasingly vociferous public, Mayor Tom Bradley formed the Mayor's Committee for Graffiti Removal and Prevention. The chairman of the committee, Stuart Haines, is the owner of Textured Coatings of America, a profitable paint manufacturing company. "It's like a guy who works in a weapons manufacturing plant being named head of a task force to stop a war," said one supporter of graffiti art.

The adult response, then, has placed top priority on eradication and enforcement of anti-vandalism statutes. Only a pittance has been funnelled into public mural programs, which give youngsters the opportunity to refine their talents under the tutelage of established artists. "The real answer is to pass tougher laws to punish the graffiti artists who deface public property, along with the gang members who are identifying their turf," says Stuart Haines.

Among the adults searching for alternatives to this deadlock is Adolfo V. Nodal, the general manager of the city's Cultural Affairs Department and a longtime supporter of public arts, via endeavors like the MacArthur Arts Project, which featured art by local writers on the park's amphitheater. "Arresting kids and abatement through paint-outs is not the only way to do it," says Nodal. "It has to be an issue of implementing cultural programs for kids. We've been fighting a losing battle on this issue."

"We haven't looked at *why* they're painting," says Mary Trotter of the Vernon Central Merchants Association, which is sponsoring a graffiti art contest that offers a cash prize of $1,200, plus wall space donated by neighborhood businesses. "They want to communicate something to us, and we're not listening."

"Hollywood should understand," says independent filmmaker Gary Glaser, who produced a documentary on the L.A. writing scene called *Bombing L.A.* "This is hype town Number One. The kids can't get on television, so they tag."

Beneath the visor of a baseball cap that barely contains his shock of bushy red hair, the sea of parking lights is reflected in Wisk's glasses. It's about nine in the evening, and we are driving east on the Santa Monica Freeway.

One of the most famous taggers in town, Wisk is a founding member of WCA. His simple but undeniably attractive tag consists of a butterfly-like *W*. He numbers every one of them, as would an artist producing a limited edition of serigraphs. The *W*s are visible as far west as Venice Beach, north to the San Fernando Valley, south to Watts and east to Pomona. After two years of almost nightly "bombing" runs, Wisk broke the 2,000 mark this week.

Blowing bubbles and snapping his wad of chewing gum, Wisk directs me to exit the Santa Monica Freeway at Crenshaw Avenue, and we park near an overpass. He opens the door a crack and shakes each of his cans, pressing the nozzles a touch to make sure they're in working order.

"Ready?" asks Wisk. He pushes his glasses back up on his nose.

We walk, real cool and slow, across the overpass to a spot of fence already bent from previous bombing raids. We slow down, even walk in place until no more cars are passing by. After a glance left and right to make sure nobody's around, Wisk says, "Go!" and we hop over the fence.

Like soldiers on maneuvers, we run low alongside the freeway wall, Wisk shaking his can all the way. We zip past sooty ivy and sickly palm trees, the roar of traffic all around us. Wisk stops about two hundred yards down from the overpass, before a spot of wall clear of bushes and trees. "Stay low, dude! Look out for 5-os and if you see one, yell out, 'Cops!'"

The can hisses as Wisk moves up and down, arcs around, outlining his throw-up in black. Then comes the fill-in, rapid back-and-forth motions with white or silver. *W*s number 2021, 2022, 2023 are up in a matter of minutes.

"Everybody takes the freeways," says Wisk, pausing before beginning *W* number 2024. "Everybody, *everybody* and their mother sees this! This is like the subways in New York, except you move past it instead of having it move past you."

Wisk, getting greedy and perhaps a bit reckless, risks a bust by going up with *W* number 2025. He's already covered fifty yards. Whatever aerosol mist doesn't make it onto the wall rises up in a cloud that is gilded by the amber street lamp above us. Wisk notices me looking at the sight. "I love it!" he exclaims, satisfaction sweeping over his freckled face.

Later, driving back down the freeway, westbound, Wisk tells me, "Look at that shit that we did the other night," pointing excitedly to his and a fellow WCA writer's tags. "Look! *W, W, W, W, J-A, J-A, J-A!* Look at all them *W*s lined up, bro'! Boom! Boom! Boom! Boom! Boom!"

"We were just kickin' it up there, drinking beer," says Skept, his freckled face and light green eyes showing the strain of the days since Prime was shot. His usual gregarious demeanor is subdued. "We were sitting down on the couch. Then, *chk, chk, BOOM! BOOM! BOOM!*"

Skept (short for "Skeptical"), a Japanese-American who grew up in a mostly Latino *barrio*, is another veteran of K2S–STN. Like Duke and Prime, he's been leading a double life for years now, although he's long since left the old 'hood and now lives in a comfortable downtown loft with his father, a well-known abstract expressionist. We walk into the ample, brightly lit studio. His father sits near the southernmost wall, smoking a pipe, poring over papers. Skept's room is at the northern end. We enter and he closes the door behind him, revealing a poster of the heavy metal group Iron Maiden.

He pops a Jungle Brothers rap tape into the player and brings out some photo albums. There's a piece by Prime, in his trademark color-patch style. And there's a photo of Geo standing before a piece, a shot taken not long before he died. He was a good-looking, slightly overweight Latino kid with a bright, adolescent smile. "Lots of friends have passed away in the last couple of years," says Skept, staring at the photo.

Then he shows me his recent work, "psychedelic" paintings on small art boards, pieces that "even my dad was surprised by." Multicolored circles, squares and bubbles appear to float in a primordial miasma. He plans on doing such a piece soon, up on a wall, perhaps here, downtown.

The question that is running through my mind as we kick back and talk about writing is, Why did Skept have to go back to the neighborhood the night the shooting took place, knowing that there was a possibility of yet another drive-by killing?

Instead I ask, "You know what adults would tell you about all this, don't you?"

"'You shouldn't go, this and that'. My dad doesn't even know I was there when they shot him. I haven't even told anybody in my family about Prime. I didn't want to hear it. I already know what they'll say."

Skept will sometimes ensconce himself in the studio, drawing for days on end. Or he'll go out piecing at the yards. Then there'll be the urge to do a daring, illegal piece on the streets. Then he'll go back and "kick it" in the old gang neighborhood. "But the shooting," I remind him.

"It's happened so many times already, I'm getting used to it," he says, then pauses. "But—I don't know why—this time it seems so different. Maybe because I was there, I was so close . . ."

"You'll go back even though you know this might happen again?" I ask.

"Probably."

A few days earlier, I had accompanied Skept, who was unshaven and had sleepless circles under his eyes, on a writing excursion to the Belmont Tunnel. Several writers were out that day, but Skept wandered off by himself to an out-of-the-way spot in the shadow of the old trolleycar station. There, he did a quick throw-up. With a baby-blue outline and a dark gray fill-in, he wrote his crew's name. The fat, blocklike letters seemed to collapse upon each other, as though plummeting through the air. In gold he wrote the names of Geo and Sine. He knelt before the piece in silence for several minutes.

Prime is sitting up in bed, flanked by two *cholos* in dark glasses. He offers his left hand in greeting. The doctors, he says, have told him that he's doing all right, "so far." He's kind of worried about their emphasis on the "so far," but says he's already going stir-crazy. He wants to go home.

He reminisces about the writing binges of the early days, when he and Skept and Geo would "walk from the Beverly Center Mall all the way downtown, tagging up all the way." They'd go all night sometimes, catching a wink wherever they could rather than go home. At dawn, they'd search for an apartment building with a swimming pool for a makeshift bath, then warm up at a local laundromat.

Prime stops suddenly. A grimace of pain crosses his face, and his right shoulder twitches involuntarily. I ask him about his arm. "I don't know, ey. I don't know," he says, looking away.

On my way out of Prime's room, I run into Duke and Radio-Tron founder Carmelo Alvarez, who continues to work closely with many of the K2S–STN writers. Duke stays with me in the hallway, leaning against the yellow wall under the bad fluorescent lights. He's working on a storefront for a neighborhood residents' association, he tells me. And he's recently been talking with Frank Romero, the famous Chicano artist. "I tripped out when he said that I could work with him on a project," says Duke, flashing a quick grin. For now, everything's "fresh."

I recall a photo Duke once showed me of Prime. It was taken on the day they worked together on a big piece near Belmont High, not far from where Prime was shot. The photo was taken looking down from the top of the wall, showing Prime frozen in mid-stroke—his right arm raised, a look of tremendous concentration on his face.

The piece they worked on that day is the one Duke is proudest of. He drew his "Dream Lady," with a soft, sensuous aqua face and windborne orange hair. Prime contributed a Cerebus-like character, K2S–STN's mascot, in baby blue, with touches of clover green and turquoise. The piece is long gone, but has been immortalized in Duke's photo album.

"If Prime comes out not being able to draw with his right hand, he'll do it with his left," Duke says with almost desperate conviction. "And if he comes out not being able to move his left hand, he'll do it with his feet."

It is difficult not to be impressed by Duke's determination. At the same time, I find myself doubting. Graffiti art is temporal, fragile. It has a lifespan of only a week or two before another writer goes over a piece, or the city buffs it out. How far can the kids really go with it? The New York gallery scene's fascination with street art only directly affected a few writers in the short time it lasted. And even if some do make it into the L.A. galleries, will their work lose its power in that context?

And what of the inner-city black hole that threatens to swallow all the colors and deny every escape route? One well-known Eastside writer was awarded a scholarship to a prestigious local art school, which he attended for three years. He's now doing time for murder. Art doesn't always save, but here's Duke before me, all enthusiasm and faith, and who's to say that he and Prime and Skept can't realize their dreams?

Later, Prime's visitors are walking out of County together, past the emergency entrance, where two paramedic trucks and a sheriff's patrol car are parked. The sun has just set and high, dark gray clouds streak across the sky, creating a dark canvas. Duke stops and stares. He has caught something we hadn't noticed: a small, baby-blue aperture in the gray.

"It's like a gateway to a new world," he says.

L.A. Journal (VI)

September 1990

> *Dear Sirs,*
> *We, the Salvadoran artists-in-exile, communicate to you our deepest concern*
> *upon the invitation extended by the Los Angeles Festival to Salvadoran*
> *writer David Escobar Galindo . . . he is a faithful representative of the*
> *ARENA government of Alfredo Cristiani, whose government is recognized*
> *as violator of the human rights of the Salvadoran people . . .*

In a conference room of a modest office building in downtown L.A., the
exiles plot revolution. The Los Angeles Festival, the spectacle directed by
Peter Sellars and billed as the event that will prove to the world once and
for all that L.A. is no longer a cultural backwater de-evolutionizing the
human race with Rambos and Valley Girls, has committed a grave error:
Galindo, poet and, according to the exiles, apologist for repressive
Salvadoran regimes dating as far back as the early 1970s, has been invited
to participate in the poetry component of the festival.

Roll call. Rigoberto "I studied with the big ones" Rey (sculptor); Roque
"Fuck the *gringos* and fuck English" Santana (poet); María "I'm really an
indígena" Virginia (writer); Pablo "Fuck the revolution, but I'm still
progressive" Paz (writer); Fidel "Orthodoxy or death" Cienfuegos . . .

¡Presentes!

The ideological spectrum sports everything from Che-in-the-mountains
true believers like Cienfuegos to social-democratic wimps like me. It is a

wonder that we can stand each other. But we do—barely. We have—for over five years now.

The draft of the protest letter (which will eventually arrive on Sellars's desk and spawn a controversy that will make the front page of the *Los Angeles Times* arts section) gets a once-over by the committee.

"*Compañero*," somebody says, "Don't you think the rhetoric is a little harsh? I mean, come on, this is 1990."

"What are you talking about, *compañero*," responds a hardliner. "Last week, we started out radical. Now you want to soften the tone of the letter. By next week, we'll be begging *them* for forgiveness!"

Eventually, the debate reaches critical mass. Shouts of "point of order!" become more frequent. And then, the inevitable, "Just what the hell is this group about, anyway?"

Depending upon the speaker, we are: (a) a perennial ad-hoc committee destined always to lag behind history by regurgitating 1960s slogans; (b) an ideologically infirm band of Salvadoran bohemians who'd rather be at one of Salvador's stunning dark-sanded beaches, drinking Pilsener (the national beer) and slurping down oysters while arguing about the whereabouts of the remains of Roque Dalton, the country's revolutionary-poet-martyr; (c) cultural workers who must stop dreaming of drinking Pilsener at the beach and reaffirm their allegiance to the Revolution so as to contribute to the forging of a New El Salvador; or (d) exiles stuck between countries, epochs, political junctures and desperately in search of a home.

It is moved that the discussion be adjourned and continued at the next meeting. Motion seconded. Unanimously approved.

Immediately afterward, a contingent of the group enters the La Tecleña, Number 3 restaurant/nightclub on Olympic Boulevard in the heart of sprawling Salvadoran *barrio* just west of the downtown 'scrapers. They ask the pretty Salvadoreña waitress for Pilsener.

"*Solo tenemos* Budweiser *y* Miller Light," she says.

A Festival of Moments

Los Angeles, September 1990

My most significant L.A. Festival moment happened in between gigs—after Peter Sellars's *Nixon in China*, before Guillermo Gomez-Peña's *1990*. I was at Música Latina, a record store in the Salvadoran *barrio*, when my companion and I heard a horrid screeching of brakes. As we walked outside, a security guard on the sidewalk yelled, "He's killed them both!" They were a young Salvadoran couple, high-school age, who'd been crossing the street when a pickup truck ran into them, tossing them into the air and down onto the asphalt. Time and space immediately expanded around us, and it seemed as if some jagged, tragic opera were taking place. Street vendors, homeless people and shoppers ran to the couple's side. Drunks stumbled out from the bars into the intersection, trying to direct traffic around the boy who now held the girl's crumpled body in his arms, screaming out her name. Witnesses ran on foot after the escaping pickup to catch a glimpse of the license plate number. Others gave chase in their cars. A large crowd gathered on all the street corners, and we waited anxiously for the paramedics to arrive. The helpless boy leaned over his unconscious, convulsing girlfriend. His screams pierced the air.

In that moment, everything that is wrong with the city was clear to me: the delayed reaction of the authorities in poor neighborhoods (police still had not arrived half an hour after the accident), a busy street in need of crosswalks (the city's poorest council district), a driver probably drunk because he's working class and has a dead-end job or no job and has booze and cigarettes crammed down his throat just like in every *barrio*.

L.A. FESTIVAL
1990

But ah, the colorful festival banners hanging from street posts all over the city: the faces of "Border Brujo" performance artist Gómez-Peña, of Thailand's Likay dancers and of the actors of El Gran Circo Teatro de Chile! The ubiquitous beauty of the Balinese fertility poles whipping in the wind above the harbor at Angel's Gate, at Griffith Park, and at the Santa Monica pier before an endless, glittering Pacific! Through the L.A. Festival, we were finally to come together, all of the L.A. cultures, in a harmonious celebration of our diversity. *Cholos* would munch Indian *garbanzo* curry alongside Cambodian refugee children alongside Santa Monica yuppies alongside African Americans . . . we would all share in each other's traditions, would be "transformed" (festival director Peter Sellars's term)—all of us, the entire city, into what we really are (can be?): a world community.

I entered the festival, the most heavily hyped cultural happening here since the 1984 Olympic Art Festival, as participant and observer, but cynical as hell. All the talk of "Pacific Rim culture" and "multiculturalism" struck me as part and parcel of the current fad through which liberal elements of the dominant culture garner government funding, present a few non-white acts but still ultimately call the shots. Cultural tourism is the term that radicals in the field use—and at times, I count myself among those radicals. *¡Hasta la victoria siempre, venceremos!*

I also was suspicious of the curatorial slant toward folkloric/traditional expressions at the big free events; the "masses" were getting mariachis and Eskimo dancers, while the avant-garde remained entrenched at the usual pricy venues. Folklore can be completely depoliticizing, the stuff that stereotypes are made of, the art that political movements of varying ideologies use to create a feel-good, uncritical atmosphere; at the same time, the vindication of certain national forms at critical historical junctures can be revolutionary. Still, the festival's fare was not so much the "mixed salad" of L.A.'s hype machine, but rather more akin to the "two-tiered" environment the city has become. Peter Sellars's dream that the ticketing computer would crash so that everyone would wind up at venues they would not normally visit did not materialize. Is it too idealistic to expect the avant-garde, "high art" and more traditional forms to be democratically accessible to all audiences? So be it: count me as an idealist.

were moments during the festival when I genuinely "got it" ... ago of the transformational seminar, used by many festival ...zers, as in, "The *Los Angeles Times* is just not getting it.") As I strolled past mariachis, surreal puppets with kids in tow, a zydeco band and a tango trio at Griffith Park one afternoon, I caught a fleeting feeling of sublime nostalgia—for what, I'm not sure, because I'd never seen anything quite like it. Maybe it recalled the rare outdoor festivals of my youth, school or church fairs where all was idyllic as an ice cream on a sweltering summer afternoon. What kept me from completely "getting it" was the makeup of the audience. Griffith Park on weekends is an eminently Latino hangout: guys playing soccer, kids waving sticks at *piñatas, carne asada* smoke wafting over the greens. Where was that crowd during the festival? Put off by the confusing traffic situation, which diverted everybody to the zoo a couple of miles away for parking? Or did the much-maligned festival publicity fail one of the communities that the festival had thought of as so integral to audience success?

At Griffith Park, as at the other outdoor sites that were to have gathered the grand L.A. rainbow coalition, I sensed something troubling about the festival's multi-ethnic earnestness—that the festival was in a sense ignoring all the class and race divisions in the city, covering up the tensions with a Disneylike It's a Small World After All theme.

But, even so, much of my cynicism melted away several times in the exhilarating and frenetic movement during the two-week event. To go from Griffith Park to downtown L.A.'s historic Million Dollar Theater on the same day, and on the next to listen to Latin American poets declaiming verse, and then on to see Southeast Asian dancers was an experience that expanded our cultural vocabulary and our own knowledge of L.A. and the places we seldom frequent. Many Angelenos discovered the festival late in the game, many others not at all. But for those who were lucky enough to attend the free gigs and many of the ticketed ones (meaning you had press credentials, festival connections or a couple of hundred bucks to burn), the breadth of the festival's breadth was undeniably dramatic.

If the festival mirrors our identity as a city, then we are as eccentric, ingenious and goofy as Peter Sellars, and we are as fragmented, schizophrenic and contradictory as the disparateness of the festival's gigs.

There was the moment at the Santa Monica Pier when a trendy magazine editor sat next to me and, with a monocle over his eye, told me how "extraordinary" the festival's inclusion of Third World exotica had been—convincing me that the whole thing was a fad that would do little more than reinforce stereotypes and patronizing liberal attitudes. But a few minutes later I didn't care, because I was completely immersed in the El Gran Circo Teatro's *La Negra Ester*, a Chilean ode to a prostitute from Santiago's *barrios*, and the nostalgia I felt at Griffith Park washed over me again, the sense that there is a larger meaning beyond the perpetual anti-romantic "now" of L.A. It is something that I feel only when I make my trips south to Mexico or El Salvador, a yearning for the time before the Fall into the cynicism that paralyzes me.

It's been a Festival of Moments. Shards of time and space, as in Japanese conceptual artist Saburo Teshigawara's often abstract but more often viscerally, excruciatingly painful yet redemptive *Blue Meteorite*, whose central metaphor is a dance over a long rectangle of broken glass before an ethereal blue panel—those shards and bodies terrify me as much as they overwhelm me with their beauty. Shards of L.A.'s identity, compacted into a two-week time frame: the tortured, possessed violence of the six bodies embracing each other in one moment and seeking blood in the next in Dennis Cooper's *The Undead*, an unblinking representation of the young gay generation's fatalism and cynicism in the face of the AIDS epidemic; the messy, claustrophobic African Marketplace, where the incense and sun dizzies me and where I can never quite figure out where the refreshments are, but it doesn't matter. This is the one outdoor gig whose audience can clearly qualify as Third World and popular, and it is fun.

Then there is Peter Sellars's own production, *Nixon in China*, where I come to admire the *Wunderkind*'s quirkiness: there is a vile Kissinger clone on stage, practically raping a young Chinese woman who comes to represent the innocence of the students at Tiananmen Square, and I am genuinely moved. And now, at the Artists' Village at UCLA, Chileans dance *la cueca* surrounded by Marlboro-smoking Cambodian dancers and young Japanese who clap along. (I turn cynical again when a Latino friend on the festival staff tells me how angry he is at the festival documentary film crew: "It's just so awful and superficial," he tells me. "They keep going around trying to set up cute shots of Aborigine children kissing Eskimos.")

I am at a post-gig party for Mexican performance artist Guillerm... Gómez-Peña, and the local Chicano intelligentsia declares war on white critics of both the *Los Angeles Times* and the *L.A. Weekly* fo... they call Eurocentric criticism that lacks validity in the Chicano... community. I vow never to write for the weekly or the Times ... Gómez-Peña on stage, plucked chickens dangling fron... alongside the US and Mexican flags. He speaks in tong..., English, quasi-*indígena* dialects—and when he says, "The misu... ...nding [between cultures] is the seed of all violence," I nod inside and out, and envision race-based battles continuing on for centuries.

Then it's the LAPD (Los Angeles Poverty Department), an artistically and politically charged local troupe of homeless actors directed by performance artists Elia Arce and John Malpede. The piece is called *Jupiter 35* and is about the harrowing experiences of Sunshine Mills. He tells of being thrown from the sixth story of a skidrow building by frustrated robbers, and then of the medieval conditions he encounters in L.A.'s public hospital. Sunshine, who is still recuperating from his ordeal, delivers the monologue from a hospital bed on stage, with his head shaved and the scars still fresh. In the re-creation of his saga, he screams, toothless, as the doctors and nurses of County Hospital talk about "lifting his face off" "just like lifting the hood of a car." "You're not a doctor!" Sunshine yells at an intern. "You're a mechanic!" The natural humor in *Jupiter 35*, the brutal honesty, high drama and process-oriented aesthetic— together made the LAPD's work the highlight of local participation in the festival.

And there are the moments of my own participation as one of the organizers of "La Raza en la Calle" at La Placita, an attempt on the part of several Mexican, Chicano and Salvadoran artists to bring *cultura popular* back to the plaza after the recent LAPD (Los Angeles Police Department) raids there. The performance would not have been complete without the police showing up once again and checking the street vendors there with us for permits. But homeless and bohemians alike were soon shouting, "*¡Que saquen a la policía!* (Out with the police!)" and, for once, *cultura popular* won out over *la cultura dominante*.

I still cringe at the clumsy choice of venue for a closing party on the last night of the festival: the Twenty/20 Club in the midst of the ABC Entertainment Center in posh Century City, where L.A.'s ethnic majority is the minority. But a short time later, we are back at the Artists' Village at UCLA, where a celebratorily drunk Japanese dancer with a Bruin sweatshirt is asking everybody to sign it in the language of their choice.

The L.A. Festival lived and died according to our glories and sins. Ultimately, I take it on its own terms. It's a "process," as the lingo goes, imperfect, superficial, deceiving, kitschy, fun, invigorating, debate-sparking. No, the city's not been transformed. But something's begun. I heard more than one festivalgoer remark, "L.A. should be like this all the time." People are envisioning a city's identity through its arts, and this is the singular, priceless legacy of the festival.

As I think again about the image that will most haunt me whenever I remember the 1990 L.A. Festival—the young girl in her boyfriend's arms, surrounded by panic-stricken street vendors, homeless people and children—I inescapably think in the next moment about Sunshine Mills at the end of *Jupiter 35*, shouting from his hospital bed, "I'm alive, goddammit, I'm still alive!"

Manifesto

Can anyone tell me what time it is?
¿O es que nadie lo sabe?
Doesn't anyone know?
¡Vamos, across the continent, North y Sur!
What time is it in downtown L.A.
when the LAPD raids the sanctuary at La Placita?
And in the city that bans santería sacrifices,
a thousand Pollo Loco stands notwithstanding?
What time is it where little Saigon meets little Havana
    meets little Tokyo meets little Armenia and we all meet
    the sea speaking in tongues?

Can you feel the earth shudder?
This generation's shaky, bro',
dancing a San Andreas cumbia!
It is 1991 and I live and die
in Guatemala, San Salvador, Mexico City
Tijuana and L.A.
This is not 1969 and Marx
has a bad rap on the international scene,
but there's the FMLN in downtown San Salvador,
(and the death squads are in L.A.)
and
¡Híjole! There goes the Berlin mauer down!

Can anyone tell me what time it is
in the great cities of the States
where Third World kids etch the walls
with a message clear
as civil war:
wildstyle, a violent
rainbow, a pistol pointed at your head!

And what time is it in L.A. when
a guatemalteco wears an Africa Now T-shirt
and a black kid munches carnitas and all
together now dance to Easy-E. and B.D.P.,
crossing every border ever held sacred?

But it's live ammunition
on the streets of Southcentral L.A.
and in Westwood and San Salvador
and East L.A.;
as real as video.

This is war, and the battle
will be block to block wherever
the Wes and Theys face off.
Third World in the First:
that's what time it is.

History is on fast forward
it's the age of synthesis
which is not to say
that the Rainbow Coalition is
heaven on earth and let's party.
This be neither a rehash of
the Summer of Love or
Fidel and Che.
All kinds of battles are yet to come
(race and class rage bullets and blood);

choose your weapons . . .
just know that everyone is everywhere now
so careful how you shoot.

Los Angeles, 1989

L.A. Journal (VII)

We're a people who walk
and walking together we'll arrive
at another city where there's no pain or sadness,
the eternal city . . .

Hymn sung by the mariachi chorus
at La Placita

October 1990

"Bring Olivares back" slurs the homeless Mexicano near the bus stop, under the shade of olive trees probably as old as La Placita itself. "What have we done to them? Why are they doing this to us?"

A few seconds before, he'd been begging in the courtyard next to the church. Then two LAPD officers were on him, pushing him out onto the street with their batons. Homeless people are gathered on the curb on the other side of the street now, watching the two white cops patrol the sidewalk. Presently they roust a street vendor who has not heeded the order to disperse.

Olivares has been gone for two months now. A couple of petition drives to have him reinstated have fallen flat: he will not be coming back to La Placita. The stirring sermons are a distant memory. Today's was offered by an aging Spaniard, in that Castilian accent that grates so harshly on the Latin American ear.

"The peace of the Lord be with you," he said. "And also with you," we mumbled. "Wait a minute," he said. "Where's the enthusiasm? This is a

SECURITY MEASURES
La Placita 1990

celebration of our faith before the Lord. He wants to see your enthusiasm, feel your energy! Louder! Say it louder! THE PEACE OF THE LORD BE WITH YOU!" "And also with you," perhaps half the parish says, slightly louder. Many don't even bother. I stop in mid-phrase.

There are newcomers to Mass these days. During today's 9 a.m. service, once offered by Father Michael Kennedy (the assistant pastor and fervent liberation theologian who also left the parish when Olivares fell ill), two LAPD officers stormed into the church in pursuit of a young homeless Latino they'd told to vacate the courtyard. In the middle of the liturgical reading, the officers chased the kid across the altar. The aging Spaniard didn't even blink. The kid escaped through a side entrance, with the cops on his heels. A few seconds later, he ran back through the church, this time down the side aisle towards the main entrance. The cops barged their way through the crowd after him. They never did catch him.

"If there's criminal activity," LAPD sergeant Barry Staggs, a barrel-chested, silver-haired man with Jesse James eyes tells me, "We're going to chase 'em right into the church or anywhere else." Staggs is standing on the grass in the middle of a small park across the street from La Placita. A few Latino couples lounge in the shade. The homeless and the vendors are nowhere to be seen. I ask him how things have been since Olivares's departure. "All that the priest did was draw criminals," he tells me. "Now, I love this," he says, his hand sweeping over the quiet and obviously uneasy couples on the grass. "You see these families—shoot. They can stay here all day long, go into the church, do anything that they want. Olivera [sic] was trying to make a political statement. And this is not the place to do it. This is where L.A. started. This was once a Mexican village, I hear. I mean, Jesus Christ," he says, mouth open and eyes wide, a look of overwrought disbelief, "here they are, all these scumbags from Nicaragua, Salvador and Honduras, every one of 'em are damn thieves. Now that it's cleaned up . . . boy, I tell ya, it's a breath of fresh air, and I feel a lot better."

A full moon rises above the downtown 'scrapers that surround the plaza across the street from La Placita. They've fenced off the kiosk tonight. Tables surround the stage and well-dressed Angelenos talk in small groups and sip wine and beer.

Father Luis Olivares is returning to La Placita for the first time since he fell ill and left the parish. It is an official affair: the dinner for "Father Louie," as he is known in activist circles, is sponsored in great part by the city itself, and the politicos are out in force. Ditto the radical chic of L.A.: progressive Hollywood actors, Left university professors, Central America solidarity activists and labor organizers (half of them dressed to kill, others—the students mostly—extremely prole). There is not a small irony to the fact that Olivares is being saluted by some of the very authorities who probably engineered his departure. With Olivares out of La Placita, gone is the figurehead of the local progressive community. And gone, once again, are the poor from La Placita. The downtown developers (who envision French restaurants and fancy clothing stores for the area) can breathe a sigh of relief.

The organizers of tonight's event thought it appropriate to put up a portable chainlink fence around the kiosk area, so that guests who paid $75 for the dinner could feast on their catered Mexican cuisine and give tribute to Olivares without the hassle of whatever homeless party-crashers are still left in the plaza area after the recent, very effective LAPD raids.

But the poor make one last stand. While a local somewhat New Age *folklórico* band does garish renditions of spacey *indígena* music (a big hit with the *gringos*), a group of poor immigrants rushes from the church shelter area up to the fence. "*¡Queremos al Padre Olivares!*" they shout. They love Olivares, they want Olivares. They can barely be heard over the sound system, but heads begin to turn.

Their fingers curl around the gray metal of the fence.

"Father Olivares helped us, economically, socially and spiritually," says one day laborer from across the fence.

Recognizing me as a journalist, the group begins to talk all at once, a collage of voices:

"The LAPD is taking us out of La Placita, they're harassing us and treating us like dogs!"

"Olivares, Olivares, Olivares," the group begins to shout in chorus.

"Tell them there's so much discrimination here. They don't care about the Constitution when it comes to Mexicanos!"

"We need another Olivares!"

"We want freedom of expression. We want the freedom to work. Even if it's just washing cars."

"The church is for everybody, not just for the rich, not just for the people who show up on TV and in the movies!"

An organizer of the event rushes over to the group. He asks me to translate for him.

"You are the people that Olivares has done all his work on behalf of . . . now, there's not much food left, but we have about thirty *tamales*."

One of the men shakes his head and stares straight at me, ignoring the organizer's liberal-guilt attack. "We're not doing this for food! We just want to tell you what's happening to us."

Their fingers poke through the chain links. "¡Olivares, Olivares, Olivares!"

But some in the group are hungry, and when the gate swings open about twenty men enter the kiosk area, with paint-flecked shoes, torn shirts and dusty hair. After being given some food, they mill about the table area. The radical chic crowd does double takes. A few get up, offering their chairs to the homeless. Some of them accept.

Olivares is introduced on the stage. A standing ovation. He has lost weight, and his skin still has a deathly pallor to it, but he walks unassisted to the podium and addresses the crowd in a voice just a notch below the one that once boomed out over the pews across the street. He recalls the words of Simeon to Mary, upon the birth of Jesus. "Behold," Olivares quotes, "this child is destined . . . to be a sign that shall be contradicted."

Generation

If I dare
to say "we,"
would it salve
the fault?
These nights fear my arrival.
So do I.
We, I mean.
I have turned over
in bed toward death
in many cities.
Everywhere, it robbed
us of bliss, of
the sight beyond
the street.
Has my generation
died yet?
It is millennium's
end,
so dance! On the freeway
spines! On the steel
breasts!
On our grave
gravel!
Can I still

sing to you,
when the news
of the day retreats?
I remember the day
that will come.
It is there,
dancing sadly, a
pauper surrounded
by machine guns.

Los Angeles, 1990

L.A. Journal (VIII)

December 1990

In a few days, I will travel south to Mexico City, to write an article about Mexican rock 'n' roll, and after yet another year-long separation, to meet Y, who is making the trip north from Guatemala. After spending a week there, we will make the trip back to Los Angeles together. We are willing ourselves back into each other's destinies, trying to rise above our fractured selves, our disjointed continent.

We've been at it for five years now (this running towards and away from each other, North and South), and our Christmasses and New Years have always been intense affairs. Last year, we visited family in San Salvador scant weeks after the FMLN offensive, breathed air that still smelled faintly of mortar dust and charred bodies, listened to the traditional Christmas Eve fireworks explode across the city at midnight: Christ reborn as missiles scream and sparks fly skyward.

A few years before, we spent New Year's Eve here in Los Angeles, celebrating at the home of Salvadoran friends. It began as a wonderful time with *abuelas* who reminisced about the old days, teens dancing, tots crawling underneath the tables. Then the shellshocked ex-Salvadoran army footsoldier in the apartment upstairs took out an automatic and started spraying bullets at enemies visible only to himself. The mothers and children screamed and everyone hit the ground. Somebody knocked over a lamp in a desperate attempt to turn off the light, and someone else crawled towards the telephone and frantically dialed the police. We were no longer in Los Angeles, but back in the middle of the war in San Salvador.

Last year, we spent New Year's Eve in Guatemala City with friends, drinking unto oblivion, setting off immense chains of firecrackers in the streets. Near midnight a friend's father lurched towards me, put his arm around my shoulder, and tried to work miracles against our inevitable diaspora: "In the year 2000," he slurred, "no matter how far we've gone away from each other, whether you're in Bangladesh and I'm in Valparaíso and my deadbeat of a son's in New York, we're all going to get back together here, *cabrón*, right here in this house, just like we're all together tonight . . ."

So this year it'll be Mexico City, the center of my universe: equidistant from San Salvador and Los Angeles, the cities/families that blur into each other for me like double vision. I need my Salvadoran fiancée here in Los Angeles, even as there is a force that urges me to be back in San Salvador. I need my cities, my families to be one.

It is during the holidays that this contradiction is always at its most intense. During this time I am usually surrounded by visions of my own death—a plane crash, AIDS, a gunshot, love, you name it—during the time that I, as a Catholic, should be thinking of beginnings, of possibilities. Instead, I am at once running into and away from my family, dying in their arms and stumbling drunk and alone, thousands of miles from home.

Tonight in Los Angeles, the houses and apartments of the *barrio* I live in are blinking with color. A glowing Santa Claus beams from the roof of the house next door. Jesuses and Marys march from house to house in the *posada* processions. *Nacimientos* adorn living rooms: *el niño Dios* lies hidden under a veil in His crèche, awaiting midnight to be uncovered. The kids are watching, as I did years ago, Dr Seuss's *How The Grinch Stole Christmas* and the Peanuts cartoon where Charlie Brown has that pitiful tree that revives only when Linus wraps his security blanket around it (always leaves me in tears, that one).

And the guerrillas of the FMLN will no doubt have a party somewhere in rebel-controlled territory, and there'll be those poignant car and plane crashes on Christmas Eve that perhaps make pointless any system of beliefs . . .

CRISTO
San Salvador

But there I will be at midnight Mass on the Twenty-fourth, back in Los Angeles after my week in Mexico City, with my fiancée at my side.

"Will one pure thing," Kierkegaard counsels. I've apparently taken the idea seriously, since here I am, trying to subdue sentimental and sexual contradiction by willing one relationship to one person for the rest of this one lifetime. Ideas of tradition and eternity beckon me as I approach thirty, after an extended adolescence of quests that celebrated ephemerality and disconnectedness.

But the doubts, the sacred doubts! Does that one pure thing ever exist outside of an isolated moment, beyond a "sign that is destined to be contradicted"? I listen to the Latin American rock 'n' roll of the old days (part of the research for the article I will be writing), reminded of the innocence of the early seventies' teenagers, thousands of whom were massacred and exiled a few years later for believing. I look down at my hands, the ones that, in a horrible, drunken fight with Y in Guatemala City a year ago, smashed the framed image of Jesus I've kept since early childhood. We'd been dreaming that we could live together in Central America . . . blood on my hand, blood on the glass, blood on Jesus.

The sign must be contradicted. Perhaps it is only through contradiction—through the death of the moment in which we will, or think we will, purely—that we may transcend our fissured reality. Like Jesus doubting in the final moments on the cross before He is delivered by the Father. We must be stripped of whatever certainty we have—pride, ego, any concrete sense of self—in order to move on to what may be the true moment of pure will (the others, perhaps, were just rehearsals in bad faith).

Somebody get me a sledgehammer for Christmas. I want to take it to the reflection of myself in those bloody shards of glass lying on Jesus's image and do away with myself spectacularly well. To be truly new, to move finally toward something/someone. While I'm at it, I'd also take that hammer to the shiny mirror glass of the malls across the city, like Jesus at the temple. Then everyone would be forced to pick flowers for presents, write poems, give embraces and make love to their enemies. We'd free ourselves from one jail, get roaringly drunk and lock ourselves into the next one.

What a time we picked to live in! The world's upside down or rightside up—I can't tell which—and we're smack in between the shattered dreams of previous generations and the abyss of the new century beyond. The holidays—symbolic markers of our passing through the world—set in motion forces impossible to contain. My uncles will be drunk, the grandmothers will wax nostalgic, you and I will embrace tensely, the fireworks will explode, the faithful will kneel, even the atheists will get sentimental, and many innocents will die. (It's already happening: a few days ago in Guatemala the army massacred a dozen people and wounded several dozen more when they fired into a peaceful procession of *indígenas* protesting human rights abuses in Santiago de Atitlán, one of the most beautiful places in the world.)

So, we'll raise a cup of wine to our lips on the Twenty-fourth at midnight, and toast to *el niño Dios* at the head of the *nacimiento* under the Christmas tree, His blanket already showing blotches of red from His omnipresent wounds.

And you and I will be trying to stop our own bleeding, uncertain whether or not we'll succeed.

Corazón del Rocanrol

Mexico City, December 1990

Under a zinc-colored sky, a block away from the railroad tracks and next to a buzzing electrical substation, a young man with hair immaculately slicked back, wearing an oversize gray jacket, a starched white shirt, a fat 1940s tie and black baggies with fob swinging low, takes giant strides as he leads me down the asphalt corridor toward the crowd ahead. "Now, you're going to see the true history of Mexican *rocanrol*!" he calls back over his shoulder, flapping along through the warm, smoggy breeze.

I scramble after him as we dive into the marketplace. Throngs of Mexico City youth in all manner of *rockero* regalia surround us: *chavas* in leather miniskirts or torn jeans, *chavos* wearing Metallica T-shirts, James Dean leather jackets or Guatemalan-style *indígena* threads. We walk past stall after rickety stall, scraps of splintered wood and twine holding up faded blue tarpaulins, where the vendors—young *punkeros* or *trasheros* (thrash fans), leathered heavy *metaleros*, Peace and Love *jipitecas* and the working-class followers of Mexican raunch-rock heroes El Tri known as *chavos banda*—sell cassettes, CDs, LPs and singles, bootlegs and imports, as well as posters, steel-toed boots, skull earrings, fan mags, spiked bracelets and collars, incense and feathered roach clips. Ghettoblasters blast Holland's Pestilence, Mexico's El Tri, Argentina's Charly García, Ireland's U2.

"*¡Tenemos punk, tenemos heavy metal, tenemos en español y en inglés, tenemos al Jim Morrison y El Tri!*" yells a young vendor, exactly as any one of Mexico's army of street vendors hawks rosaries or Chiclets. His is but one voice among hundreds at El Chopo, as the sprawling swap meet is known.

It's a Saturday afternoon, some ten years after this institution was born, and the vendors tell me that the crowd of about three thousand is on the light side. "What's *chingón* is that there's no divisions here between the different *rockeros*," proclaims Ricardo, a high-school kid in a T-shirt emblazoned with the logo of the punk band LARD, a Vision Streetwear beret and hip-hop hi-tops. "It doesn't matter whether you're hardcore or *trashero*."

Mexican authorities haven't distinguished between styles either: all are equally suspect. El Chopo is often raided by police eager to club skinheads and longhairs alike, Ricardo and his young punk friends say, as a *jipiteca* strolls by with a gleaming white Fender Precision bass, telling everyone that he'll let it go for one million pesos.

It isn't long before my zoot-suited guide is recognized. "Don't you play with la Maldita?" kids inquire, before asking for autographs. Roco, the lead singer of Maldita Vecindad y los Hijos del Quinto Patio (roughly, The Damned Neighborhood and the Sons of the Tenement) greets all comers effusively. "And don't forget to make the gig tonight! At LUCC, about midnight! '*¡Ahórale, hijo!*'"

We're already hopelessly late for a meeting with Maldita's manager on the other side of the city (a trip that takes about an hour and a half by subway and bus), but Roco is intent on getting me freebies. Already I'm loaded with copies of *La Pus Moderna*, one of the city's underground magazines, along with more than a dozen LPs and cassettes by groups with names like Atóxxxico, Sedición, Psicodencia.

"It's the craziest city, *hijo*," Roco says, standing in place for a rare moment before a stall featuring a lithograph of Marilyn Monroe hanging next to another of Che Guevara. "Anything can happen here."

"We've received influences from all over," he adds, the words spilling out rapid and vowel-twisted, in classic Mexico City, or *chilango* slang. "From the North, from the South, from Europe. It might be true that rock began in the North, but now it's all ours."

"Rock *en español*," reads the publicity slogan, "Music for a New Generation." Since the mid-1980s, in Mexico, Argentina and Spain, *rocanrol* has been billed as the perpetual Next Big Thing. Record labels, mostly the Spanish and Latin American subsidiaries of majors like BMG,

Sony or WEA, signed dozens of bands. Stadium gigs drew huge crowds at most of the big capitals in Latin America.

Key groups lived up to the advance publicity: Mexico's Caifanes, a dark-pop band reminiscent of The Cure, sold a respectable 100,000 copies of their first album; a subsequent *cumbia* rock single, "La negra Tomasa," moved half a million. Other acts, such as Radio Futura and La Union from Spain, Los Prisioneros from Chile, and Miguel Mateos and Soda Stereo from Argentina, sold well and garnered airplay throughout Latin America.

Impresarios also looked toward the USA and its relatively untapped Latino youth market: there have been impressive Latin-rock gigs in Los Angeles and other major American cities since 1988. "L.A. is a meeting ground for rock from Latin America and Spain," says Enrique Blanc, a deejay at Rancho Cucamunga's KNSE, one of the few Spanish-rock supporters in the States. "And there are plenty of people with money who are interested." Marusa Reyes, a transplanted *chilanga* producer living in Los Angeles who handles both Caifanes and Maldita Vecindad, succeeded in convincing Jane's Addiction to book a few shows with a special added attraction: none other than Maldita Vecindad y los Hijos del Quinto Patio.

Roco and the Chopo crowd want to shake Mexican culture down to its very roots. But these heavier *rockeros* are still on the margins—and not because they necessarily like it there. It's the pop rockers like Menudo that have become megastars. As one veteran of the Mexico City rock wars put it, "The joke here has always been that *this* is the year real *rocanrol* is going to make it—and we've been saying it for thirty years."

In the summer of 1985, a group of *chavos* from different Mexico City *barrios* began holding jam sessions: a piano player, a vocalist and six percussionists (water bottles, pots and pans), but nothing experimental about it. "Either we waited to save up and buy equipment, or we played with what we had," recalls Roco, his leg bouncing nervously up and down on the bar stool.

The city around them was on its knees, again, enduring the worst economic crisis since the revolution of 1910. A profound malaise contaminated all areas of life. Then, on the morning of September 19,

1985, Mexico City lurched over its liquid foundation, the ancient volcanic lake it was built upon.

"It was total devastation, *cabrón*," Roco says, leaning into me and yelling over UB40's "Red Red Wine." "Whole *barrios* darkened, without electricity, water running everywhere, people carrying coffins, looking for their loved ones. The people of the *barrios* had to organize themselves to survive. All of a sudden, people I'd seen my entire life but didn't know, I knew."

Citizens' committees organized relief efforts much better than the government, which had spurned international aid for the first two days after the quake, claiming it had "everything under control," until a second devastating *terremoto* made it clear that nobody controlled anything.

The city was transformed by the experience. Out of the rubble there arose all manner of new populist political personalities, including Super Barrio, a masked wrestler, whom the earthquake turned into an activist/performance artist who to this day shows up in his yellow cape and red suit wherever slumlords do their foul deeds. Cuahutémoc Cardenas nearly tossed the ruling PRI (Partido Revolucionario Institucional) dynasty out of office (something that may yet happen). In the midst of this upheaval, Maldita Vecindad y los Hijos del Quinto Patio were born.

The other members of La Maldita join Roco and myself at our table, weaving through a crowd whose attire would fit in well in New York's East Village or on L.A.'s Melrose Avenue. These *niños bien* have paid 50,000 pesos (about $17) for Maldita's *tocada*, their gig. We're in the Zona Rosa, the Pink Zone, at Rockstock, a club whose logo bears a suspicious resemblance to the Hard Rock Café's.

In comes Pato, curly locks peeking out from under his trademark gray fedora, a veteran of several vanguard Mexican bands. Sax, at twenty-two the youngest of the group, is leaning toward a U2 look with long, straight hair and loose, gauzy white shirt. He's Maldita's purest musical talent, and moonlights with mariachi bands in the famous Garibaldi Plaza. Lobo, a dark, leathery *rockero*, is the quiet one who batters the congas. Elfin-smiling and clean-cut Aldo, born in Argentina but now a full-fledged Mexico City boy, is on bass. And Pacho, the oldest at twenty-nine, with head shaved close on one side and exploding curly on the other, is the drummer, an intellectual who studied anthropology at Mexico's finest university, UNAM. (Roco, too: he's finishing his degree in journalism.)

La Maldita huddle close together sipping Coronas and smoking Marlboros in Rockstock's cagelike no-smoking section. Their look—resonances of James Dean, Tin Tan (a Mexican comedic great of the 1940s and 1950s, who popularized a Chicano/Pachuco swing style), U2 and the Mexico City *barrio* kids of Buñuel's *Los Olvidados*—clashes wildly with that of the surrounding scenesters. Roco's wearing a pair of mammoth black work boots. He notices me eyeing them.

"They're just like my father's, *cabrón*," he says, lifting his foot up and inviting me to tap the steel toe. "They cost sixty thousand pesos, *cabrón*—not like those European ones that all the *niños bien* wear, that sell for three hundred thousand here in the Zona Rosa.'

Maldita and other young bands, like Café Tacuba, Santa Sabina and Tex Tex, lash out at the Americanization of the Mexican middle class, a tendency led by media giant Televisa. This corporation prides itself on nationalism, a tune that's made it millions and that the PRI government has also used to help keep itself in power for the last seventy years. It's a bastion of national pride, but Televisa is also accused of promoting "*malinchismo*", a term that goes back five hundred years to La Malinche, Hernán Cortés's Aztec translator, the most famous traitor of Mexico's history.

Televisa's is a no-lose strategy: by backing both national and *gringo*, mainstream and underground, it's cornered all markets. But somehow, the Americanized acts always seem to fill the screen. Pato tells the story of the time Maldita did *not* meet Madonna at L.A.'s trendy Club Vertigo. Seems that somebody told somebody that Madonna was in the club the night of the band's first L.A. appearance. Though the band members swear they never met her, tabloid headlines hit home instantly—the blonde goddess had given the sons of Mexico her blessing. Upon returning to Mexico City, the band was deluged with press queries about their all-night party with Madonna.

"They wanted to know about her, nothing about us," recalls Aldo. Horrified, the band called a press conference to set the record straight. "But it made no difference," Aldo says, finishing his beer before he heads backstage. "They still ask us about her all the time."

MALDITA VECINDAD

When Maldita bounds on stage, they start without so much as a hello. They play with a precise fury, styles merged, overturned and burned. Ska gives way to funk, funk to rap, rap to *son veracruzano*, to *danzón*, to *cumbia* and mambo on one of their anthemic numbers, "Bailando":

> *No tengo ni puta idea porque quiero hoy salir*
> *lo ultimo de mis ahorros me lo gastaré en ti*
> *en la fabrica dijeron, "Ya no nos sirves, Joaquín"*
> *para no perder dinero nos corrieron a dos mil*
> *hoy es viernes por la noche todos salen a bailar*
> *yo me apunto en el desmoche tengo ganas de gritar:*
> *¡Ya no aguanto mas, quiero bailar!**

A few kids sing along, some skitter perfunctorily about the dance floor. It seems the *niños bien* don't want to risk tearing a thread. But Roco doesn't care: he's bouncing up and down, splaying his legs like Elvis being chased by *la migra*, diving down and nearly kissing the floor with the mike stand. His face flashes a grin, a sneer; now he jerks his head back repeatedly, as though he's being slapped by interrogators, while rapping his way through "Apañon," a song about police abuse of *barrio* youth:

> *En un sucio callejón, despiertas sin recordar*
> *nada de lo que pasó, te duelen hasta los pies*
> *no traes dinero no traes zapatos y ya no traes pelo*
> *sales de ese callejon, ¡ODIANDO!***

Jesus, I'm thinking, Maldita have blasted on the wind of free-jazz sax past decades of balding folk trios, put the lie to the World Beaters by merging mambo, *danzón*, R & B, ska and rap—within each song—exploding it all on stage with the rage and rapture of boys possessed by the most sacred of

---

*I don't have a fucking idea why I want to go out tonight/but I'll spend the last of my savings on you/at the factory they said, "We don't need you anymore, Joaquín"/they fired two thousand so as not to lose any more money/it's Friday tonight, everyone's going out to dance/sign me up in the madness, I really want to scream:/I can't stand it anymore, I want to dance!
**In a dirty alley, you wake without remembering/anything about what happened, even your feet hurt/you don't have a jacket, you don't have money you don't have shoes and you don't even have hair/you leave that alley, HATING.

rock demons, and these kids (black-stockinged *chicas*, Mel Gibson *chavos*) aren't seriously dancing?

When Maldita's roadies begin to break down the equipment, UB40's "Red Red Wine" again blares through the speakers. Suddenly, five hundred Zona Rosa kids are singing along in English, dancing so cool.

While the *niños bien* pride themselves on their Americanized hipness at Rockstock, elsewhere in the city a bunch of long-haired, wannabe *gringo* kids from Tampa, Florida, are playing before another crowd, having been billed as death-metal heroes from the North. On Televisa, surely, there is a fake blonde reading the news off a prompter. And all across the city on billboards and posters hung in liquor stores, buxom blondes are tonguing beer bottles, sucking cigarettes. Looks like La Malinche is alive and well and as sexy as she was five hundred years ago.

> *Yo lo único que quiero hacer*
> *es bailar rocanrol . . .* *
>
> Los Locos del Ritmo, circa 1960

The battle for the cultural soul of Mexican youth may well be as old as La Malinche. And Mexico City intellectuals are only half joking when they say that postmodernism actually originated here five hundred years ago, with the Conquest and its clash of radically different sensibilities. The tango, swing and mambo have each arrived from distant lands and transformed the city's style. Even so, most of what was promoted on radio, vinyl and the silver screen through the first half of the century was the sacred *cultural nacional*—mariachis and romantic balladeers like Augustín Lara or Pedro Infante.

When the first leather jackets and Elvis pompadours appeared on the streets of the *barrios*, the over-forty guardians of culture, nervous that Mexico City youth would arm themselves with switchblades and roar Harleys through elegant Zona Rosa establishments à la Marlon Brando in *The Wild One*, mounted an all-out assault. Films like *The Blackboard Jungle* were pulled from

*The only thing I want to do/ is to dance rock & roll . . .

movie theaters and newspapers apprised the populace of the dangers of *rocanroleando*: gang violence, lax morality, and, especially, the destruction of *la cultura nacional*. Maybe the single thing the government, the Catholic Church and the Marxist left could all agree on was that Mexican youth was imperiled by the Protestant, decadent and individualistic North. But *bandas* like Los Locos del Ritmo, Los Apson Boys, Los Hooligans, Los Crazy Boys and Enrique Guzmán y los Teen Tops all had avid followers.

Most songs from the early years were covers sung either in English or awkwardly translated into Spanish ("Hotel Descorazonado," "Rock de la carcel," "Pedro Pistolas," "Un gran pedazo de amor"). Gradually, however, the translated covers of American hits became more than literal adaptations; Mexican *rockeros* began rewriting the lyrics. "Under the Boardwalk," for example, became "En un café". While these tunes were often fluff, the feel of the songs was subtly shifting toward a Mexicanness that, many years later, would come to exemplify the best of the country's rock.

Lest the Old World version of *cultura nacional* be forever buried, the *oficialistas* made one final attempt to crush the *rockeros*. Elvis Presley, undisputed king in 1957, was their weapon. In what was probably an unsubstantiated story, Elvis was quoted in a border newspaper as saying, "I'd prefer to kiss three Negro women than one Mexican."

Headlines across the country. "¡INDIGNACION POR INSULTO A LAS MEXICANAS!" "¡INICIA FUERTE BOICOT CONTRA EL INSOLENTE ARTISTA!" Radio stations sponsored massive public record-shatterings. "Love Me Tender" was yanked from playlists. But, as Federico Arana, Mexico's premier rock historian, points out in his *Guaraches de ante azul* (Blue Suede *Guaraches*), the conspiracy was bound to fail.

"The best that you can do for a person or group to reaffirm their ideals is to persecute them and surround their lives with prohibitions," writes Arana. "The story of the three kisses actually helped Mexican *rocanrol*."

> *Ayer tuve un sueño, fue sensacional*
> *los pueblos vivían en paz . . .*[*]
>
> Los Pasos (Spain), circa 1970

[*]Yesterday, I had a dream, it was great/all the nations lived in peace . . .

In the late sixties and early seventies, rock reached into every corner of Mexico, Central and South America as more bands bypassed covers and explored the peace and love idealism of the time, with original songs in Spanish. In Mexico, rock had become a solid underground christened *la onda*, or "the wave" (a term that survives today in all manner of colloquial speech: "*¿Qué onda?*", "*¡Que buena onda!*").

In 1971 at Avándaro, on the outskirts of Mexico City, anywhere between one hundred thousand (government figure) and half a million (*rockero* version) *chavos de la onda* attended a two-day festival featuring bands like Three Souls in My Mind, Love Army and El Ritual. The spectacle was a mirror image of Woodstock, right down to one of the organizers stepping up to the mike and warning the kids about a bad batch of LSD. The authorities braced for a predicted riot, but the *rockeros* camped out peacefully under the rain with little food or warm clothes and, yes, plenty of pot and acid.

"The fact that so many kids got together in one place really scared the government," recalls Sergio Arau, who later formed Botellita de Jerez, one of the most important bands of the eighties. The government had every reason to be nervous. It was the first large gathering of youth since 1968, the year the army massacred several hundred protesting students in the Tlatelolco district of Mexico City. Since Avándaro, the Mexican government has rarely granted permits for large outdoor rock concerts.

For Carlos Monsiváis, one of the Mexican Left's best-known essayists, *la onda* still seemed more of an imitation of the North's hippie culture than an authentic national discovery, except in one important regard. "*La onda* was the first movement in modern Mexico that, from an apolitical position, rebelled against institutionalized concepts [of culture]," he writes in *Amor perdido*, a collection of essays on the sixties in Mexico. "And it eloquently revealed the extinction of cultural hegemony."

Throughout the early seventies, *jipitecas* wearing *guaraches*, loose sandals with auto-tire soles, hitchhiked across Mexico on hallucinogenic pilgrimages, a tattered copy of *Las enseñanzas de don Juan* stuffed into their rucksacks. Even Joaquín Villalobos, today the top commandante of El Salvador's FMLN guerrilla army, admitted that there is room for *rocanrol* in *la revolución*—probably half the cadres of any given guerrilla army listened to groups like Los Pasos in the mid-1970s, not to mention Pink Floyd and Led Zeppelin. Salvadoran Marxist friends have boasted to me of sneaking a few tokes of pot and listening to rock on battered tape recorders, breaking away from clandestine military training on El Salvador's remote beaches.

By the early eighties, however, Mexican rock was on the verge of extinction. Only a handful of Mexican bands survived the doldrums of the late seventies—punk hadn't arrived to save *rocanrol* here as it had in the North—and El Tri, formerly Three Souls in My Mind, was the only solid draw. The battle between English and Spanish, North and South, had been virtually conceded to the *gringos*. The city had a bad case of Saturday Night Fever.

After generations of *rockeros* had done their best to overthrow the *cultura nacional* by singing in English and bleaching their hair, it took a few radicals to discover the obvious—that they didn't need to go north to take back rock-'n'-roll. Botellita de Jerez announced the birth of a new sound: "*Guacarock*" (*guaca* as much a reference to *guacamole*, the sacred national snack, as to *guacatelas*, an onomatopoeic term for vomiting). Botellita reclaimed popular traditions like the *norteña* and *cumbia*, as they ridiculed American rock megaheroes and *el PRI*. Mexico City youth were joining their cultural roots with the heart of rock-'n'-roll.

Considering how well these worlds merged, one begins to wonder whether rock is really foreign to Mexico City at all. Ask Roco, and he'll say that the blues could have begun only here, what with the city's deep ties to Afro-Caribbean culture, its long-standing love affair with death. And rock itself? Where else could it have exploded into being other than in the biggest city in the world, where soot and sex and social unrest are legendary? Even rap: Roco claims the music actually originated in Mexico with Tin Tan and fellow golden-era comedian El Piporro. "Just listen to the raps on the streets of the city," he says. "The vendors are the best rappers in the world!"

After Botellita, frenetic movement ensued: hardcore punk (Atóxxxico, Masacre '68), industrial disco rap (Santa Sabina), roots rock (the perennial El Tri and younger bands like Tex Tex), dark pop (Caifanes), straight pop (Neón, Fobia, Los Amantes de Lola), and bands like

Maldita and Café Tacuba, with their crazy blends of styles from North and South—all churning out Spanish-only product.

"There was an explosion," says Luis Gerardo Salas, executive director of Nucleo Radio Mil, a network of seven radio stations in Mexico City, one of which is dedicated full-time to rock. "Everyone in Mexico seemed to want to be a *rocanrolero*. People discovered that there was rock in Spanish with the same quality as in English."

The *hoyos fonquis*, underground clubs that spontaneously appeared in poor neighborhoods, were the heart of the new scene. Bands would set up in the middle of the street, running electricity straight from somebody's living room. "All of a sudden, you'd see smoke rising around the stage," says Lalo Tex, lead singer of Tex Tex. "But it wasn't from a smoke machine. It was the dust being kicked up by the kids dancing on the asphalt."

A childlike awe overwhelms me as we pull up to the block-long monolith that houses the biggest media conglomerate in Latin America. We walk past the security checkpoint and wait in an antiseptic hallway. I glance at a pair of memoranda on the wall: one says you'll be fired if you're fifteen minutes late, the other urges employees to attend a seminar entitled "How to Enhance Your Image." Tonight Maldita enters Televisa's domain, for a live appearance on Galavisión, a cable infotainment network.

To be inside the monster, finally! After nearly three decades of watching it in my Mexican grandmother's bedroom in Los Angeles: all those macho heroes and child stars, Jacobo Zabludowsky, the dour-faced anchor with the Mickey Mouse earphones, and Raúl Velasco, variety show host with the sweet "This is our glorious national culture" voice. Zabludowsky and Velasco are among the most powerful men in Mexico, friends to presidents and corporate executives the world over.

Though it is often considered synonymous with *el PRI*, Televisa may be more powerful than the party. It is one tentacle of the country's most powerful business cartel, the Monterrey Group, which owns over 90 percent of television outlets, numerous radio stations, an important record label, and, to boot, the country's biggest brewery. If you want to reach the masses, Televisa is the only way.

Maldita lounge about smoking cigs, antsy to get the performance over with. "Our real audience is in the *barrios*, at the universities," Pacho says, a little defensively. So entering into the realm of Televisa is a contradiction, right? "We aren't just going to do Televisa's bidding—we aren't about that," he scoffs.

The Marxist youth of the sixties and seventies would never have walked through Televisa's glass doors—except with machine guns. Even today, some look upon *rockeros* like Maldita and Caifanes (who have been on several Televisa shows) as *vendidos*, sellouts. Maldita insist that reaching the mass audience is crucial. But what will happen on the day that they decide to sing a song, say, about political prisoners on a Televisa program? Or burn the Mexican flag? Or use profanity on a single?

While the anchors read the news off prompters a few feet away, the band takes its place on the pristinely waxed stage, before elegant bronze urns gushing water. The newscast breaks for a commercial and, a few seconds later, on a talk-show set at the other end of the studio, entertainment hosts Rocío Villa García and Mauricio Chávez (she an aging, tall fake blonde in a red dress, he a light-complected innocent in preppy sweater and black tie) shuffle papers and listen to the countdown. "And now, with us tonight is a group of fine young men . . ." The studio fills with a loud recording of the only song that's gotten airplay, "Mojado," the tale of a father who makes the perilous journey to the USA but dies along the border "like a pig, suffocated in a truck." These tragic lyrics are set, somewhat bizarrely, to a blend of highly danceable tropical and flamenco rhythms.

Televisa staffers crowd the plate-glass windows that seal off the newsroom, watching the band make an only half-serious effort to lip synch to the recording. Restrained at first, Roco begins jumping tentatively, but it's not until the second song, the Veracruz-style "Morenaza," that the band really loosens up. Sax spreads his arms and snaps his fingers, twirls about. Pato sneers, scratching ska-ishly at his guitar. Pacho and Lobo are bashing away on percussion—which, apparently, you're not supposed to do when lip-synching—you can hear the skins being pummeled even above the deafening monitors. Aldo plucks his bass with a vengeance. And Roco is now all over the waxed floor, collapsing his legs, flailing them outward in a leap, skidding and sliding . . . this image is being seen live all over Latin America and Europe, I'm thinking, but twenty minutes from now, it'll be back to the soap operas and wheezing professors discussing the Aztec legacy. And then I notice it: from the moment he hit the stage, Roco's black work boots (just like his father's) have been scuffing the Televisa floor like jet tires on a runway. Rocío Villa García is drop-jawed in horror. Technicians are making exaggerated hand signals, trying to settle Roco down. But no! Roco is blind to the world, on the verge of knocking himself out dancing as the song slowly fades.

Out bounds Villa García, all smiles for the interview. "Roco," she bubbles, "just how is it that you can dance around with those *heavy* boots?" Roco looks down at them, and for the first time notices the dozens of black streaks radiating out from his mike. Before he can answer, Villa García is already into her next question.

"Now just what is this about Madonna showing up at your concert in Los Angeles?"

In the late 1980s, encouraged by the success of such Argentine *rockeros* as Soda Stereo and Charly García, as well as by the birth of *guacarock* in Mexico, the labels began signing again. BMG's Ariola led the way, producing Mexican acts Los Caifanes, Maldita Vecindad, Fobia, Neón and Los Amantes de Lola. A suspiciously supportive Mexican government also helped by allowing a few rock acts from Argentina to stage large outdoor gigs. At the Plaza de Toros in 1987, twenty-five thousand *rockeros* attended the biggest *rock en español* gig since Avándaro.

In 1988, the hit that promoters, label execs, radio program directors and *rockeros* had all been waiting for arrived: "La negra Tomasa" by Caifanes. The song was a slightly electrified, *cumbia*-style cover of an old Cuban standard, and it sold over half a million copies—more than any other Mexican single in the thirty-year history of *rocanrol*. It seemed as if rock's Latin hour had finally come.

Not quite. No other band came close to matching the sales of "La negra Tomasa": most acts topped out at well under 50,000 units. Maldita barely managed 25,000. "There was a crash," says Jorge Mondragón, a Mexico City rock promoter. "People were saying that *rock en español* had only been a fad."

The reasons cited for the crash were familiar: bad label promotion, unscrupulous concert promoters, conservative radio, government censorship.

"Let's face it," says Giselle Trainor, an Ariola label manager. "It's not as easy to sell this concept as it is to sell Lucerito." The teen star's voice is nonexistent, but her long legs and fair hair have made her a Televisa darling. "And if other labels don't start supporting rock, it's going to collapse."

Soon after the initial boom, pop rockers like "Mexican Madonna" Alejandra Guzmán (daughter of Enrique Guzmán of Los Teen Tops, the *rockero* heroes of the sixties) achieved stardom, propelled by Televisa's massive promotional machine.

"Rock was taken over by people who aren't *rockeros*," says Nucleo Radio Mil's Gerardo Salas. "Sometimes I think that the whole *rock en español* movement was planned and promoted in such a way that pop rockers like Timbiriche and Menudo would end up winning."

Pop rock, one Televisa promoter told me, is most successful with the middle class, Mexico's strongest consumer force, and the bulwark of the PRI. Working-class *chavos de la banda*, who are more likely to listen to the underground, are not part of the equation. "They're dirty, violent," I was told by the promoter, who complained about violence at *hoyos fonquis* and at some of the few larger scale concerts (a violence, *rockeros* say, that is usually provoked by the authorities). "The underground may just as well roll over and die. We don't want to have anything to do with that crowd, and we never will."

Bouncing around El LUCC, a dingy concrete vault light-years away from Rockstock in the south of the city, Roco has his arm around Saúl Hernández, lead singer of Los Caifanes, slurring: "Come on, *cabrón*, admit it. You guys sound like The Cure. *Ya no mames, güey*." And Saúl comes back, rocking back and forth on his heels: "Not everything has to be so obvious like in your songs. There's an interior landscape, too, *cabrón*."

By the time Maldita stumbles onto the stage, the walls of the club are sweating. Everyone's hair is pasted onto their foreheads in the dripping-wet air. I inch my way through the crowd, slipping on stray bottles on the unseen floor below. The balconies seem on the verge of collapse, dozens of kids hanging over the railing.

The sound coming from the stage convulses, lurches: Roco, Sax, Pato, Aldo and Lobo are floating away on tequila-inspired riffs (they've been partying since early afternoon), steamrolling crazily toward a great abyss, drunk boys daring each other as they look down into the darkness and laugh. The anarchy doesn't perturb the crowd in the least. On the dance floor a thousand bodies match Maldita's wild energy leap for leap.

Roco loses his breath during the melodramatic held note on "Morenaza." Sax stumbles through solos, barely keeping up with the rushed rhythms, flapping across the stage in his loose shirt, waving his arms, giggling. Lobito is oblivious of everything but his own private torpor, slamming away at bloodied congas (he ripped his hand open during the second song).

Punkish youths leap on stage and tumble back into the crowd. Now Roco himself takes a diving leap of faith into the mass of steaming bodies. Now Sax. Now Roco is pushing Pato, guitar and all, into the pit.

The band launches into "Querida," a hardcore cover of pop megastar Juan Gabriel's hit. Roco leaps skyward so high that he bangs his head on the red spotlight overhead. Saúl Hernández suddenly climbs onto the stage in all his tall, dark elegance, plays with a microphone-become-penis between his legs, hugs Roco like a long-lost brother, throws his head back, closes his eyes, and then without warning he too dives out onto the dance floor, where the slamming youths edge ever closer to absolute madness.

As the crowd files out afterward—punks, ex-hippies, ex-Marxists, kids from the *barrios*—Lobo is nursing his hand, bleary-eyed in the arms of his girlfriend. Aldo is downing more beer at the bar. Pacho, the only one who played the gig straight, is talking with a small group of fans. Roco is nowhere to be found. Sax is back behind the percussion section, weeping into a friend's arms—in a few minutes he'll make a bizarre attempt at taking off his pants and pass out.

Tonight, Maldita have fallen apart. Tomorrow they'll wake up, hungover as hell, in the city where *rocanrol* never quite dies.

L.A. Journal (IX)

June 1991

Was that a shotgun? In answer, a series of pops . . . a small automatic? I crouch by the window, look into the hazy balmy night. Mute buildings. Now, from afar, another sound begins, like the whine of a mosquito in the darkness of a stifling room in the tropics. The whine becomes a roar that rattles the windows. A shaft of light pours down from the sky. Sirens shriek in the distance. They come closer . . . closer: patrol cars race up the avenue.

I am not in San Salvador, I tell myself. Those are not soldiers down there, bursting through doors to ransack the apartments of high school kids who participated in a protest march . . . Y is okay, she works for a human rights organization in Los Angeles, she's not FMLN in San Salvador anymore, this is Los Angeles, not San Salvador, this is 1991, not 1979, this is gang strife, not civil war. I don't believe myself. Images past and present merge: It is 1979 and 1991 and San Salvador and Los Angeles and gang strife and civil war all at once.

When the helicopter's thud-thud-thud-thud fades away, I light a cigarette. Did the bullets find their mark in a rival gangster, a three-year-old's skull? I wait for the ambulance's siren, but the neighborhood remains quiet. The bullets found nothing but the night, as though the night itself were both target and victim of the desperate rage that led the finger to pull on the trigger.

I return to my post next to the computer, in my Echo Park apartment (my latest stop in search of a home) whose living room holds my altar.

Amidst votive candles and before a crucifix, I've gathered together objects from the living and the dead: a wallet-sized photo of Y, her stare questioning me across the distance of our latest—and final?—separation; on a cassette sleeve, a photo of Mexico City kids who look like a cross between Irish idealists U2 and the street toughs of *Los Olvidados*; a black-and-white snapshot of a graffiti artist cradling his brutally scarred arm, result of an evening when the bullets did find their mark; a brittle, yellowed leaf from Palm Sunday at La Placita, where Father Luis Olivares showered the thousands of Mexicanos and Centroamericanos surrounding him with holy water; the embossed card that says that one Fidel Castro Ruz, *Presidente del Consejo de Estado y del Gobierno de la República de Cuba*, requests my presence at a reception; a rather ugly postcard entitled "La Frontera, Tijuana, BC," that shows an antiseptic-clean highway on one side and a labyrinth of dusty paths on the other . . . shards of my identity, scattered like the beads of broken glass strewn across the Golden State Freeway three miles north of here, where a big rig hauling fifty thousand pounds of tomatoes crushed a trailer home, killing three of four members of a tourist family who had come all the way from Canada to visit Disneyland—it's a newspaper clipping from the *Los Angeles Times* stuck to my bulletin board, in between a Dodgers baseball schedule and a 3-D postcard depicting the Crucifixion.

This jumble of objects is as close as I get to "home." As close as I get, because my home is L.A. and L.A. is an anti-home; that's why I've left it so many times, and returned just as many. Taking to the road, I've crossed and recrossed the border heading south and north—trying to put things back into place the way they were before . . . before what? The civil war? My grandfather's heart attacks? The gangland massacres? My father's alcoholism, the Latin American dictatorships, my first failed love, the treaty of Guadalupe Hidalgo?

I turn off the overhead light so that the candle flame transforms the shadow of the crucifix on the wall into a pair of wavering, reaching arms. I gaze upon the photos of my late grandparents. This is my history, I tell myself. "This is my home," I whisper, looking out through the window again at the avenues of Echo Park, which are now as deserted and tense as any in San Salvador during a state of siege.

Laid out in not-so-neat little piles before me, there are photos and

PRAYER BEFORE DINNER

La Placita 1989

manuscripts and cassettes that contain the ghost voices of the dead, next to my omnipresent moving boxes. It is as if I have a city lying about me, no, as if there were cities strewn across my living-room floor: a history aglow in the wavering candle flame. I reach behind one of the votive candles atop my late grandparents' old 78 r.p.m. console and pick up a small, splintered piece of *bahareque* that I brought back from El Salvador five years ago. I look closely at the dried mud that still clings to the thin, bamboo-like wood. It is from the frame of a house that no longer exists. A house that collapsed.

VINTAGE DEPARTURES

A Wolverine Is Eating My Leg by Tim Cahill

Journeys through Himalayan rapids, the Grand Terror of Montana, and Dian Fossey's forbidden zone, all told with a special blend of sharp insight and crazed humor.

"Irreverence is a specialty of Tim Cahill's generation, and he ranks among its apostles."
—*Washington Post*

A Vintage Original/Travel/Adventure/0-679-72026-X/$11.00

The Road From Coorain by Jill Ker Conway

A remarkable woman's exquisitely clear-sighted memoir of growing up Australian: from the vastness of a sheep station in the outback to the stifling propriety of postwar Sydney; from untutored childhood to a life in academia; and from the shelter of a protective family to the lessons of independence and tragedy.

"A small masterpiece of scene, memory...this book [is] the most rewarding journey of all."
—John Kenneth Galbraith

Autobiography/0-679-72436-2/$10.00

The Good Rain: Across Time and Terrain in the Pacific Northwest
by Timothy Egan

Traveling from rain forest to English garden, mountain top to river gorge, the Seattle correspondent for *The New York Times* reveals the Pacific Northwest as a land of both unparalleled beauty and frenzied exploitation.

"A celebration of natural bounty, a warning that too much has already been lost . . . Egan is a worthy spokesman for his homeland, a fluent and crafty writer."
—Richard Nelson, *Los Angeles Times*

Nature/0-679-73485-6/$10.00

Bad Trips, Edited and with an Introduction by Keath Fraser

From Martin Amis in the air to Peter Matthiessen on a mountain top, some of the best-known writers of our time recount sometimes harrowing and sometimes exhilarating tales of their most memorable misadventures in travel.

"The only aspect of our travels that is guaranteed to hold an audience is disaster. . . . Nothing is better for self-esteem than survival."
—Martha Gellhorn

A Vintage Original/Travel/Adventure/0-679-72908-9/$12.00

Motoring With Mohammed: Journeys to Yemen and the Red Sea
by Eric Hansen

A fascinating introduction to a land of haunting ancient customs and terrifying modern-day politics, as well as unparalleled desert beauty.

"Picaresque, beguiling, and great fun."
—Diane Ackerman, *The New York Times*

Travel/Adventure/0-679-73855-X/$10.00

The Lady and the Monk: Four Seasons in Kyoto by Pico Iyer

Through Pico Iyer's search for the traditional Japan of flower arranging and the silence of temples, he discovers a modern land as comfortable with rock music, shopping malls, and Vivaldi as with classical Japanese literature and tea ceremonies.

"A beautifully written book about someone looking for ancient dreams in a strange modern place."

—Los Angeles Times Book Review

Travel/Adventure/0-679-73834-7/$12.00

Running the Amazon by Joe Kane

"The story of the first expedition to run the entire length of the Earth's longest river . . . a terrific adventure . . . a torrent of stories from the first dusty road to the final champagne drunk at the Atlantic."

—Los Angeles Times Book Review

"Kane's eloquence lends his story a you-are-there quality."

—Cleveland Plain Dealer

Travel/Adventure/0-679-72902-X/$9.95

Looking for Osman: One Man's Travels Through the Paradox of Modern Turkey by Eric Lawlor

As he traverses Turkey in search of exotic splendor recorded by nineteenth-century romanticists, Eric Lawlor finds instead a modern, professional, sometimes brutal land, with unexpected remnants of the old Turkey to be encountered along the way.

A Vintage Original/Travel/Adventure/0-679-73822-3/$11.00

A Year in Provence by Peter Mayle

An "engaging, funny and richly appreciative" (*The New York Times Book Review*) account of an English couple's first year living in Provence, settling in amid the enchanting gardens and equally festive bistros of their new home.

"Stylish, witty, delightfully readable."

—The Sunday Times (London)

Travel/0-679-73114-8/$10.00

Into the Heart of Borneo by Redmond O'Hanlon

An account of the 1983 journey into the heart of Borneo by a British naturalist with the knowledge of a trained scientist and the wit of a born comic writer.

"Within this intrepid travelogue lies the soul of Monty Python.... Every misstep of the way, O'Hanlon employs a dry, self-deprecating style that cannot disguise [his] gift for fresh and arresting description."

—Time

Travel/Adventure/0-394-75540-5/$11.00

The Road Through Miyama by Leila Philip

A beautifully perceptive look at the cultural roots of Japan, as seen through the eyes of a young American woman who spends a year in a small southern village as an apprentice to a master potter of a centuries-old craft.

"As perceptive and evocative as Japanese *haiku* and a delight to read."

—Edwin O. Reischauer

Travel/East Asian Studies/0-679-72501-6/$9.95

Iron & Silk by Mark Salzman

The critically acclaimed and bestselling adventures of a young American martial arts master in China.

"Dazzling . . . exhilarating . . . a joy to read from beginning to end."

—*People*

Travel/Adventure/0-394-75511-1/$10.00

Low Life: Lures and Snares of New York by Luc Sante

In this "fascinating. . .entertaining and sobering" (*Philadelphia Inquirer*) journey through New York City, from 1840 to 1919, Luc Sante discovers the dark heart, wherein dwell pimps, madams, rat-killing dogs, ear-chewing thugs, con men, and extravagantly crooked cops.

"*Low Life* captures the rollicking atmosphere of city life. . . .Sante reclaims an essential piece of the city's past."

—*The New York Times Book Review*

History/Sociology/0-679-73876-2/$14.00

In the Shadow of the Sacred Grove by Carol Spindel

A moving memoir of an American woman's difficult and gradual acceptance into the daily life of a rural West African community.

"I was unprepared for the quietly gathering power of this respectfully inquisitive study of modern life in a small West African village. It poses, and answers, questions about the lives of a proud and shy people."

—Alice Walker

A Vintage Original/Travel/Adventure/0-679-72214-9/$12.00

You Gotta Have Wa: When Two Cultures Collide on the Baseball Diamond by Robert Whiting

An American journalist gives us a witty close-up view at *besuboru*—Japanese baseball—as well as an incisive look into the culture of present-day Japan.

"[It] will please baseball fans and enlighten anyone interested in Japanese-American relations."

—James Fallows, *Atlantic Monthly*

Sports/Current Affairs/0-679-72947-X/$12.00

Available at your local bookstore or call toll-free to order: 1-800-733-3000.
Credit cards only. Prices subject to change.

VINTAGE DEPARTURES

___ *One Dry Season* by Caroline Alexander	$10.95	0-679-73189-X
___ *The Emperor's Last Island* by Julia Blackburn	$12.00	0-679-73937-8
___ *Fast Company* by Jon Bradshaw	$6.95	0-394-75618-5
___ *Maple Leaf Rag* by Stephen Brook	$7.95	0-394-75833-1
___ *Among the Thugs* by Bill Buford	$12.00	0-679-74535-1
___ *Road Fever* by Tim Cahill	$10.00	0-394-75837-4
___ *A Wolverine Is Eating My Leg* by Tim Cahill	$11.00	0-679-72026-X
___ *The Heart of the World* by Nik Cohn	$12.00	0-679-74437-1
___ *Coyotes* by Ted Conover	$11.00	0-394-75518-9
___ *Whiteout* by Ted Conover	$11.00	0-679-74178-X
___ *The Road from Coorain* by Jill Ker Conway	$10.00	0-679-72436-2
___ *In Xanadu* by William Dalrymple	$13.00	0-679-72853-8
___ *Danziger's Travels* by Nick Danziger	$15.00	0-679-73994-7
___ *The Good Rain* by Timothy Egan	$10.00	0-679-73485-6
___ *Bad Trips*, edited by Keath Fraser	$12.00	0-679-72908-9
___ *Samba* by Alma Guillermoprieto	$11.00	0-679-73256-X
___ *Motoring with Mohammed* by Eric Hansen	$10.00	0-679-73855-X
___ *Native Stranger* by Eddy Harris	$12.00	0-679-74232-8
___ *One for the Road* by Tony Horwitz	$6.95	0-394-75817-X
___ *The Lady and the Monk* by Pico Iyer	$12.00	0-679-73834-7
___ *Video Night in Kathmandu* by Pico Iyer	$13.00	0-679-72216-5
___ *Shooting the Boh* by Tracy Johnston	$11.00	0-679-74010-4
___ *Running the Amazon* by Joe Kane	$9.95	0-679-72902-X
___ *Making Hay* by Verlyn Klinkenborg	$9.00	0-394-75599-5
___ *In Bolivia* by Eric Lawlor	$8.95	0-394-75836-6
___ *Looking for Osman* by Eric Lawlor	$11.00	0-679-73822-3
___ *The Other Side* by Rubén Martínez	$10.00	0-679-74591-2
___ *Toujours Provence* by Peter Mayle	$10.00	0-679-73604-2
___ *A Year in Provence* by Peter Mayle	$10.00	0-679-73114-8
___ *The Panama Hat Trail* by Tom Miller	$11.00	0-394-75774-2
___ *Last Places* by Lawrence Millman	$10.00	0-679-73456-2
___ *All the Right Places* by Brad Newsham	$9.95	0-679-72713-2
___ *In Trouble Again* by Redmond O'Hanlon	$11.00	0-679-72714-0
___ *Into the Heart of Borneo* by Redmond O'Hanlon	$11.00	0-394-75540-5
___ *Holidays in Hell* by P.J. O'Rourke	$12.00	0-679-72422-2
___ *Paris Dreambook* by Lawrence Osborne	$10.00	0-679-73775-8
___ *The Village of Waiting* by George Packer	$12.00	0-394-75754-8
___ *The Road Through Miyama* by Leila Philip	$9.95	0-679-72501-6
___ *Iron & Silk* by Mark Salzman	$10.00	0-394-75511-1
___ *From Heaven Lake* by Vikram Seth	$11.00	0-394-75218-X
___ *In the Shadow of the Sacred Grove* by Carol Spindel	$12.00	0-679-72214-9
___ *The Voyage of the Sanderling* by Roger D. Stone	$12.00	0-679-73178-4
___ *Fool's Paradise* by Dale Walker	$7.95	0-394-75818-8
___ *You Gotta Have Wa* by Robert Whiting	$12.00	0-679-72947-X